THE
HAPPINESS
MANUAL

THE HAPPINESS MANUAL

A GUIDE TO YOUR DAILY SELF-MASTERY

STAS ARSONOV

NEW DEGREE PRESS

THE HAPPINESS MANUAL

A Guide to Your Daily Self-Mastery

ISBN   978-1-63676-814-4   *Paperback*

          978-1-63730-228-6   *Kindle Ebook*

          978-1-63730-258-3   *Ebook*

To my friend, Jamil

CONTENTS

—

INTRODUCTION

———

When I was a kid, I loved to walk outside after it rained. There were always so many rainworms on the ground. I remember one day I asked my grandma where they come from, and she replied, "They fall from the sky with the rain." A few decades later, when I was in college, my buddy Koby and I walked outside in our neighborhood after it rained, and there were all these rainworms on the ground. I remember looking at them and exclaiming, "Man, it blows my mind how these worms just fall from the sky with the rain!"

Then there was a long pause, and both Koby and I burst into laughter. That silly interaction turned out to be the pivotal moment that started my quest to awakening. It was my "aha" moment that shed some light in the room for me to look around and ask myself, *What other beliefs did I take for granted?* One of such inquiries was about my understanding of happiness.

Various ancient sages, spiritual teachers, and modern transformation coaches have attempted to help us understand that happiness is not a destination, but rather a journey. We do not need to achieve new career heights or live in an ashram. Happiness is available to us today, right now.

Applying this revelation is a lot easier said than done. You may need to hear it a million times before you finally embrace this idea. Many people spend their entire lives looking for happiness before they finally understand that it was there all along. The good news is that you can access the happiness that resides within you at any given moment. It's just a matter of learning how to clear the obstacles that stand in your way.

A recent study by Dr. Jordan Poppenk and Julie Tseng from Queen's University in Canada revealed that we could have over six thousand individual thoughts per day. Close to 95 percent of those thoughts are the same repetitive thoughts, and 80 percent of those have a negative connotation.[1] A significant share of these thoughts is us dwelling on the past or wondering about our future. We spend lots of energy worrying about problems that, most of the time, never actually happen.

Instead of focusing on practices that can help replace these negative thinking patterns with more empowering ones and ultimately helping us live a more joyous life, many people try to earn their way to happiness. They may say, "I'll be happy after this next promotion, meditation retreat, a trip to Spain, or an Ayahuasca ceremony."

---

1   J. Tseng., and J. Brian Poppenk, "Meta-State Transitions Demarcate Thoughts Across Task Contexts Exposing the Mental Noise of Trait Neuroticism," *Nature Communications* 11, no. 1 (July 2020): 1-12.

Unfortunately, the premise that we have to earn happiness assumes we are not good enough the way we are. We feel the urge to continually achieve, accomplish, and accumulate experiences and things to be happy. Slogans like "I'll sleep when I'm dead" motivate us to keep moving forward without pausing to consider whether our actions make us any happier. The problem with limiting beliefs like "happiness has to be earned" is that very few people question them.

There's an inspiring parable about an elephant and a rope that illustrates the power of such conditioning. In this story, a giant elephant is held captive by a small piece of cable tied to his front leg. The elephant never tries to escape because this rope was tied to him when he was still very young, and it held him in place. The grown-up elephant can obviously snap it in seconds and walk away, but he never attempts to do so because he is conditioned to think he can never break away. That's why it's crucial to contemplate the beliefs we take for granted that may no longer serve us but actually hold us back in life.

Like many other people, I believed happiness had to be earned. I've spent a good portion of my life attempting to improve and master myself so I could finally deserve the right to be happy. In the last five years, I've spent over $200,000 trying to build the best version of myself. I attained degrees and certifications, worked closely with mastermind coaches, spiritual teachers, personal trainers, psychotherapists, intuitive healers, shamans, astrologers, health coaches, and even pursued the biohacking route and spent a ton of money on innovative procedures. All of this was done with one goal in mind—to attain happiness. To become good enough.

Finally, after I had failed and suffered enough, I went to see my meditation teacher, Scott, and told him that I was ready to give up my pursuit of happiness. I told him that I had dedicated so much time and money to get to that blissful state, but I didn't feel like I was getting any closer. That's when he explained to me something fundamental about happiness. "Happiness is not something that comes upon us like a state of euphoria and permanently remains. It has to be generated from within every single day," Scott said.

That moment, I realized that happiness was a conscious decision; a way of life. All of us deserve to be happy, and we are able to generate this state of being every day in the various aspects of our lives. As you will find in the chapters ahead, there are many ways to cultivate happiness.

Do we focus on what's wrong with the world, our lives, and ourselves, or do we pay attention to all of the beautiful things instead?

Are we unconsciously attempting to control relationships with our loved ones, or do we accept them as they are?

Are we feeding our bodies and souls with nourishing elements?

Freeing ourselves from the limiting beliefs we've accumulated over the years can help us see things clearly without labeling them as good or as bad. Not blaming others for how we feel and taking more responsibility for our inner state can become a clear path to evoking happiness more regularly in our lives.

After that realization, I started taking more responsibility for my inner state, which helped me attract exceptional people and exciting opportunities into my life. I let go of pursuing careers that seemed excellent on paper but made me miserable inside and instead launched ventures that excited me. With the support of some talented people, I filmed a short documentary about selfless acts of kindness. This opened me up to helping others and authentically expressing myself.

I also launched the *Think Clever* podcast, where I interview fascinating guests in the field of personal transformation. I met and learned from motivational speakers, spiritual teachers, social activists, and thought leaders to better understand how they pushed beyond their comfort zones and to hear what awaited them on the other side. And of course, since you are reading this, I have published my first book.

I experienced a vital shift in my physical and mental health. Most importantly, I *rewired* many limiting beliefs that held me back from experiencing happiness. I realized it's not always enough to say, "I choose to be happy." There are rituals and lifestyle changes that can help you get to that state of well-being. I made it my mission to discover those tools and apply them to my life. There are many benefits to discovering the happiness that is already accessible to you. In this book, I hope to show you:

- How to derive more satisfaction from life and create daily rituals for a successful day;
- How to have a better relationship with yourself and the people around you;

- How to experience more satisfaction and fulfillment from the work that you do;
- How to take responsibility for your thoughts, emotions, reactions, and actions; and
- How to release limiting beliefs that hold you back from reaching your full potential.

The *Happiness Manual* is for people who want to experience more clarity throughout the day and make better decisions in life. It's for those who want to have a more conscious life and live with intention. It's for the seekers who want to co-create with the Universe and manifest the life they dream for themselves. It's for people who want to be happy. If you are holding this book, perhaps it's for you.

CHAPTER EXERCISES

I didn't want this book to become another inspirational self-help read that you put down, feel great for a few days, and start wondering what's next on your reading list. The goal of this book is to support you in creating a new experience for yourself. The only way to do that is through active participation. At the end of each chapter, you will find exercises designed to help you apply some of the information you just read. Most of them will invite you to write things down, so it may be a good idea to start a journal where you can record your observations.

Your teachers can guide you to the door of self-discovery. They can even help you pick out the right key. You have to be the one to open that door, though, and walk through it. That's how you discover your insights—a shift to a perspective you weren't aware of before. An insight happens inside of you; it becomes your inner truth. Nobody can gift it to you, because it will be just a piece of information. You have to discover it through your own experience. When you do that, you'll start experiencing life from a very different viewpoint.

CHAPTER 1:

WHERE ATTENTION GOES, ENERGY FLOWS

———

"You create your thoughts, your thoughts create your intentions, and your intentions create your reality."

—WAYNE DYER

In 2016, I shut down my swimwear company and embarked on a self-exploration journey. I spent the next few years traveling around the world, studying with spiritual teachers and various experts in the field of personal development. I attended one retreat after another, discovering valuable insights along the way but still not finding the answers I searched for. I remember participating in a seminar by Kyle Cease and discussing ways to make our world a better place when, all of a sudden, I snapped. I grabbed the mic and unleashed everything that had been weighing on me for years. I said, "There is so much darkness in the world: people killing each other every day, kids dying from starvation, corrupt leaders, a polluted planet, extinct animal species... none of it is getting better despite all of the amazing spiritual teachers we have in the world."

I finished my outpouring of thoughts by simply stating that sitting down to meditate would not change anything in the world that day. Kyle had a different view of this situation. He invited me to change the lens I used to look at the world. He said, "Stas, I can see that you've been focusing a lot on what's wrong with our world and finding examples of that. Why don't you try something different and focus on all of the beautiful things in the world instead?"

Kyle's suggestion reached me at a perfect time. I had heard it so many times and in so many different ways that, finally, the puzzle pieces came together. I realized I was the only one responsible for what I invited into my life and what I chose to focus on. As the great saying goes, "Where attention goes, energy flows."[2] I believe this exact wording was first attributed to James Redfield, but the essence of this instruction has been shared by many teachers around the world.

I decided to try something different and focus on all of the beautiful things. I committed to surrounding myself with people dedicated to spreading love and kindness around the world. The events that followed, and ultimately this book, are the result of this pursuit. I set out to meet amazing people who lived their lives by a completely different set of principles; who operated from an abundance mindset. If they wanted to experience more kindness in their lives, they

---

2   James Redfield, *Celestine Prophecy* (Boston: Little, Brown & Co., 1994).

spread it around them. If they wanted to receive more love, they gave love. I didn't have to wait long until the Universe presented me with an opportunity to spend some time with a person like that. His name is John Pogachar, and he started the *LOVE on Every Billboard* movement.

LOVE on Every Billboard

It all began with just one billboard in Spokane, Washington. The word "love" spelled out in big white letters on a red background. No hashtags, no links, just LOVE. Soon, over 127 LOVE billboards popped up in the United States, Russia, Canada, Ukraine, New Zealand, and Austria. Hundreds of millions of people have come across these billboards and experienced their healing effects. For some people, they served as a reminder that they are loved. For others, the billboards reminded them to be more loving with the people around them.

This movement did not start in a brainstorming session of a digital marketing firm; rather, by John going in nature and patiently listening to silence. He grabbed his backpack and went into Kings Canyon National Park in California to camp. As he sat among the sequoia trees, he contemplated what he could do to spread more love around the world. He began to wonder what would happen if he just put the word "love" in huge letters on a billboard.

John asked himself if this was too big of an idea for him and if he was even up for such a task. He was sixty-two years old, retired, and did not have any experience starting a social activism movement. He was within his comfort zone and was not ready to leave it quite yet, so he wrote down the idea on a napkin and stashed it in his pocket. Then, gradually, he started seeing the word "love" pop up everywhere he went. He saw it on the streets, on displays, on T-shirts, even on a rock. Finally, John realized this idea was more important than staying in his comfort zone and feeding his doubts, so he used a substantial part of his savings and rented a billboard for a month.

The following day he shared his vision to put LOVE on a billboard with his coaching group. He told them he had already paid for one to go up in his hometown of Spokane, Washington. Right away, people on the call were inspired by John's altruistic act and wanted to support him on his journey. They offered to send donations and share his information with their friends. The only problem was that John never had a PayPal account or any social media.

That's when the power of the community showed him he was not alone. People volunteered to create a landing page for him, a PayPal account, and social media profiles within just a few days. John's ability to receive allowed others to give. They contributed their time, resources, and skills. People wrote songs about LOVE billboards, invited John to podcast shows, and made short documentaries about the impact of this selfless act.

John maintained the momentum of expanding by letting go of any hesitation he had about starting a movement. For him, the main ingredient was to make sure that everything happened organically and with lots of joy. When I interviewed John about his experience, he said that his motto was, "Let's just play and see what we can come up with." John defined his success not by how much money he made, but by the lives he touched and impacted in a positive way. And in that sense, he was a multi-millionaire.

So much has happened because John Pogachar listened to his inner calling that day in the woods and because he took a leap of faith and did something different. "I had a choice to sit there in my apartment, go have coffee every day, and talk to the same people, or I could do something totally different. I chose to go into the unknown and go see what's out there," he said.

The world has become a lot friendlier for John, and all of a sudden, he had many friends in several cities across the globe. He drastically expanded his network filled with like-minded individuals who had similar purposes in life. They invited him to visit, and he took another leap of faith and gave up his apartment in Spokane to drive across the United States and visit the cities with LOVE billboards. I think one of John's talents that makes others want to be his friend is his ability to look for the best in people. Most importantly, he recognizes people's efforts to become better and contribute to the world. He plants good seeds wherever he goes.

John Pogachar reminds me of a character from a short story written by French author Jean Giono called *The Man Who Planted Trees*. It's an inspiring story of a man who found a desolated land where nothing grew. People left that land a long time ago, but the man saw something special there. He envisioned that it could become a lovely place with a delightful community. For years he planted seeds in the dirt every single day. One day, a young fellow traveled through that region and witnessed what that man was doing. He thought the man had lost his mind. Nothing grew there, yet he kept planting seeds. Decades went by, and the young man came back to visit. To his surprise, this abandoned land transformed into a beautiful forest with a friendly town nearby. Animals returned, and life was beautiful once again.[3]

A Very Kind Place

When Kyle Cease invited me to shift my focus to all of the beautiful things in the world, he mentioned that the transformation I was seeking would come from turning my attention away from myself. Kyle's seminar was the third personal growth event I signed up for that month. The deeper I went, the more areas of improvement I discovered within myself. I was obsessed with transformation and attended one workshop after the next. It seemed that as soon as I fixed one problem, I encountered another one. It was a vicious circle of trying to fix and heal myself in order to feel whole and worthy of happiness.

Kyle's proposal opened me up to making myself available to other people. I started to wonder how I could be of service to others and offer my help. Fortunately, I didn't have to wait long. When John Pogachar announced he put up a billboard with the word LOVE on it, something deep inside me told me I needed to capture that story and help John spread the message. The very next day, I called up my friend, Koby Poulton, and asked if he wanted to come with me to Spokane,

---

3   Jean Giono, *The Man Who Planted Trees* (Boston: Shambhala, 2000).

Washington, to film a story. Luckily, he said yes, and it turned out to be one of the most memorable experiences of my life.

Spending time with John and interviewing people who drove by the LOVE billboard allowed me to forget everything I was worried about before. My insecurities, anxiety, and depression took a backseat, because it wasn't about me anymore. The story had to be told, and I volunteered for the task. I had zero experience making documentaries and interviewing people, but here I was giving it everything I had. We interviewed regular people for this film—store owners, factory workers, and anyone who passed by the LOVE billboard. I had no idea what kind of reaction to expect from them. Quite frankly, I thought that some people would treat it as a joke and not pay much attention to it, but that was not the case. The feedback we received made me realize the significance of this movement even more.

For instance, I asked a car mechanic, Mike, about his impression of the billboard right in front of his shop, and he said that the town needed a reminder to slow down and notice one another. Another store owner said he felt a bit disconnected from people, and seeing the LOVE billboard on his way to work helped to uplift his mood. It turned out to be just what the people of Spokane needed at that time—a reminder to be more loving to each other and to show support. Our experience working on this project inspired us to call this film *A Very Kind Place*.[4]

---

4   Stas Arsonov, "A Very Kind Place: The LOVE Billboards," June 27, 2019, produced by Stas Arsonov and directed by Angel Isabel, video, 10:07.

What If Kindness Was Cool?

Another love and kindness pioneer who helped me see the world as a beautiful place was Dr. Jeremy Goldberg. Jeremy worked on his PhD in marine biology conservation and sustainability and spent his days in a cubicle. Life was comfortable and stable, but he felt it was eroding his soul. It wasn't how he wanted to spend the next forty years of his life. Jeremy knew he couldn't go on this way and needed to do something unconventional.

In our interview, Jeremy said, "If you want to do something different, you have to be someone different. You have to leave the comfort and security of the nest you've created with your normal life. And you have to step toward the unknown, uncertain future that you are trusting is the right way forward."

In 2010, Jeremy stood at the airport gate, waiting for his flight to board. He looked over and saw a woman crying by herself. He wanted to do something to help her, so he reached into his wallet, pulled out a card, and wrote on the back of it—*It'll be okay, and you will be too.* He walked over to her, looked her in the eyes, handed her the card, and went to board his flight.

He didn't know what her reaction was but hoped that her life got a little bit better at that moment. In an instant, he realized that there was an honor in helping someone get through the day. During his flight, Jeremy wondered why a woman was left to cry by herself while surrounded by a crowd of people staring at their phones. Why was he the only one who came forward to help her?

Jeremy started thinking about whether this was the kind of world he wanted to live in. He pictured an alternative version of this reality where the same lady was crying, only this time she was bombarded with support. He imagined an older man walking over and hugging her. A group of teenage girls, stopping by to sing her a song. He pictured a couple on their honeymoon coming over and inquiring if she was okay and telling her a joke.

He recognized that such a world was possible. As he sat on the plane that day, he imagined a world where kindness was natural and acceptable. A world where helping a stranger was not an exception. Rather, that it was expected. That day he decided he was going to make a difference in the world. In his TEDx Talk, "What If Kindness Was Cool?" Jeremy said, "I didn't know where to start. But I had a passion, and everything starts with passion. So I sat on the plane, and I pictured what a kindness revolution would look like. And I decided that it would look like any other type of revolution. And that we would start with an idea whose time has come, and ideas are just words. So I thought that I would start there, with words."[5]

Everywhere he went, he started leaving little *love bombs*, notes of kindness and support. Jeremy began to write articles online, and people started sharing them with their friends. And now his words had been shared hundreds of thousands of times, all around the world. Jeremy created a community

---

5   Jeremy Goldberg, "What If Kindness Was Cool?" Filmed May, 2015 at TEDxTownsville Townsville, Australia, video, 17:19.

of connections; a community that shows the world is filled with good people doing good things.

He started by giving a crying stranger a hint of hope, and now he gets thousands of messages from people telling him how he inspired them, lifted their spirit, and helped them get through their day. For the last decade, Dr. Jeremy Goldberg has been on a mission to make kindness cool again. He gave a TED Talk, published a book, and launched a *Long Distance Love Bombs* podcast to spread love and create a world where kindness is cool.

I genuinely believe that we are in charge of the experience we invite into our lives and that we get more of what we focus on. If we focus on everything' wrong with the world, we will undoubtedly find proof of that. If we focus on all of the beautiful things in the world, we will also find evidence of that. So why not choose to invite more kindness and love into our lives? Read on to discover how to apply that in your life.

CHAPTER EXERCISE:
WHAT DO YOU WANT TO ATTRACT INTO YOUR LIFE?

What do you focus on throughout the day? Do you find yourself visualizing your goals coming to fruition, or do you mentally replay a comment someone made that hurt your feelings? Write it all down in your journal. Make a list of five things that keep popping up in your head regularly. Examine them. If they happen to be thoughts about what you're not doing right, see if you can flip them around and focus on the desired outcome instead. For example, in place of saying, "I don't read enough or I don't have time to read," reframe it to

"I read once a week, and I would like to start reading more." Instead of focusing on everything you don't have, list all of the things you would like to have or how you would like to feel. Place your attention on what you want to happen in your life.

It's important to stay realistic about where you are at this stage of life and how you feel. You can't fake it 'til you make it. If you take this route, you may end up living in a fantasy world, continually tricking yourself into some altered state. Let's say you're not happy about being single. It won't help fooling yourself with positive affirmations like *I don't need anyone, I'm fine on my own.* It will not match how you actually feel and instead will generate internal resistance and suffering for you. That's why it's crucial to acknowledge what you're dealing with and then develop a game plan on how to move forward. Acknowledge where you are, and then write down what you would like to attract into your life and how you want it to look.

CHAPTER 2:

DAILY RITUALS

———

"You'll never change your life until you change something you do daily. The secret of your success is found in your daily routine."

—JOHN C. MAXWELL

"You're an extraordinary well-digger!" exclaimed my meditation teacher, Scott, as I arrived for one of our sessions. "You have mastered the craft of digging wells. As soon as you finish one of them, you move on to the next one. But the problem is that they are all empty, Stas. There's no water in them."

The *water in the well* is a reward for our commitment. It's okay to explore different practices and study with various teachers, but eventually we need to make a choice and commit. That's when we start seeing our well begin to fill with water. Ask yourself the following question, What do I struggle with the most? If you struggle with fatigue, stress, fear, anxiety, brain fog, or procrastination, consider that these states may linger around throughout your life. You may never be able to get rid of them once and for all, but you can develop a ritual to help overcome these unpleasant states whenever they emerge.

When it comes to building your practice, your own ritual, start with your *why*. Why are you doing it? What is it that you want to get out of it? Let's say you want your ritual to help you reduce stress. Dig deeper and find out why do you desire that. Perhaps when you feel stressed out, you make unfavorable decisions at work or yell at your kids at home. That's something you'd like to change about your life. So, what you really want from your ritual is to help you make better decisions at work and be more loving and kind around your family. That's your *why*. Now when you wake up in the morning and think about skipping your workout or meditation practice, you will remember the real reason why you chose your ritual, and it will be much easier to stay with it.

Committing to a ritual makes the difference between a professional and an amateur. Professionals don't leave it up to chance to be *in the zone* and make rewarding decisions. Instead, they take control of their inner states with the help of their rituals.

For example, one of my mentors, Bo Eason, a former NFL player turned playwright and keynote speaker, rolls out his feet with a stone before every public speaking appearance to stay more grounded and mindful of his body language. Tony Robbins, the world's top motivational speaker, jumps on a mini-trampoline before his events to stimulate the lymphatic system and raise his energy levels. Wim Hof, also known as the "Iceman" for his ability to withstand freezing temperatures, regularly takes cold showers to train himself to get out of his comfort zone and strengthen his mind-body connection.

Just as you brush your teeth every morning to keep them cavity-free, your rituals should be second nature to you. It's an ongoing effort to grow and to assume more responsibility for your inner state. Remember that it takes time to establish a ritual that can help you achieve your goals. You have to be willing to show up every day, set an intention, and be clear on the direction you're headed.

I used to be a total passenger in my body whose productivity depended on my mood that day. My strategy for getting my energy levels up was loading up on coffee and chewing gum. Once in a while, I went to a breathwork or a meditation class, saw an energy healer, worked out at the gym, and took my supplements, but I didn't have a clear plan on how to manage my inner state.

Finally, I decided that it was time to get into the driver's seat of my life and stop leaving my day's success up to a chance. I challenged myself to commit to just one practice and stick with it for the next thirty days. There was a lot to choose from, but I decided to settle on breathing exercises. As soon as I woke up, I headed straight for my yoga mat and began my daily ritual.

Practicing breathwork first thing in the morning helped me bring more oxygen into my brain and kick-started my entire nervous system to start the day right. As time went on, I began to feel more focused, energized, and excited. However, it wasn't just about the stimulating effects of breathing; it was also the result of me finally taking matters into my own hands. I started assuming more control of my emotional state by committing to a consistent ritual that enabled me to set the tone for the day as soon as I woke up.

It requires discipline to build a consistent practice. Over the last few years, I went through many variations with my daily rituals. Some techniques proved to be very helpful, and I still apply them every day; others I only use as needed. Nevertheless, having all of these tools in my kit made me more confident about facing challenging situations and taking charge of my life. Below are some of the practices that have positively influenced my life and were or still are a part of my daily ritual.

Breathwork

Breathing is one of the most powerful tools, yet it's overlooked by many people. It seems like an obvious thing to do, but you'll be surprised how often people lose control of their breath during intense situations. Breathing brings oxygen to your brain so that you can focus on goals and make favorable decisions. When you focus on the breath, you can better control your emotions and choose how to respond in challenging situations. In a recent study of mindful breathing and anxiety, Kangwon National University researchers concluded that conscious breathing decreases anxiety and substantially increases automatic positive thoughts.[6]

---

6   H. Cho, S. Ryu, J. Noh, and J. Lee, "The Effectiveness of Daily Mindful Breathing Practices on Test Anxiety of Students," *PLoS One* 11, no. 10, e0164822 (October 20, 2016).

My teacher, Scott Schwenk, uses breath as a powerful tool for healing and transformation. During his classes, he implements an ecstatic breathwork technique to help his students enter an altered state of consciousness and to release old tension patterns that might cause them pain and suffering. Ecstatic breathing utilizes breath to help equalize the energy within the body. "One of the biggest gifts of working with the breath is that anything I could possibly have stuck in me is not about the story. It's the energy that's lodged in my nervous system that needs to get digested, and breath does that invariably," said Scott.

In his interview with Jeff Krasno from *One Commune*, Scott shared a story about a profound transformation he experienced during his very first breathwork session and how it had changed the trajectory of his life.[7] It happened about fifteen years earlier, when he had visited a gentleman named David Elliot, who later became one of his teachers. When Scott asked him what he should expect from the session, David replied that he would focus on getting him out of his head and into his heart. They talked for a bit longer, and Scott got on the massage table and began the breathing exercises.

"It was like lightning was coursing through my body, no kidding. Like somebody had plugged me into the wall, and 220 watts were flowing through me. I had never felt the intensity of energy that profoundly. The tears started to come. I felt this huge opening in my heart, and it was that clarity; it was that feeling of revelation," Scott shared.

---

7   Jeff Krasno and Scott Schwenk, "Open Your Breath, Open Your Life," February, 2019, in *Commune* podcast, audio, 29:00.

When he sat up after the session, Scott knew that this was the path he wanted to pursue. Breathwork unified all of the healing modalities and spiritual teachings he had learned over the years. These days, Scott uses an ecstatic breathwork technique to help people address various physical, emotional, and spiritual issues. Breathing became Scott's ritual to generate his inner state every day.

Meditation

A practice that withstands the test of time is, of course, meditation. There is a reason why so many people adopt it as their primary practice. Some meditate to reach enlightenment, while others do it to help them manage stress or tap into their creativity. Studies have shown that meditation can have positive benefits against an array of both physical and mental conditions. The bottom line is that I have never met a person who recommended staying away from this practice.

Meditation helps slow down the continuous stream of thought and make space for something greater to come through. It's a practice of *being* rather than *doing*. Meditation is about doing less—less thinking, judging, comparing, complaining, and assuming. It's about observing how our minds attempt to seduce us to engage in those distracting activities but brushing them off to remain focused on the silence within.

One of the most challenging activities for me was to sit in silence and meditate. In the beginning, it was hard to accept this as something productive. I remember just sitting there, not feeling anything, and walking away disappointed and skeptical, but returning to my meditation cushion again and again. When I let go of the expectation of something miraculous happening while I had my eyes closed, I experienced a shift in my perception. It was so subtle that it took some time to realize something within me had changed.

I became more deliberate and started thinking twice about my words and my actions. The practice of observing my thoughts during meditation transformed into a habit of observing myself throughout the day. It was especially helpful during stressful situations when I could have said something hurtful, but I didn't because I focused on my breath instead and let the moment pass.

There are many types of meditation that you can practice, and it's probably a good idea to try a few different ones to see which one works best for you. However, don't make it too complicated so that it prevents you from building a consistent practice. You don't have to go to a yoga studio and sit in a perfect lotus position to meditate. It's accessible to everyone. You can meditate on the bus or even on your couch. Just look for the space between your inhale and exhale and try to rest there for as long as you can.

Gratitude Journaling

I experienced another shift in my consciousness when I began a gratitude journaling practice. Each day I listed three things for which I was grateful. No matter how lousy or how glorious my day was, I always had something to be thankful for. I discovered an appreciation for the smallest things in life and for seemingly random encounters. I started looking at the world through a lens of gratitude and appreciation, and as a result, I received more experiences to enjoy.

So much is happening around us simultaneously, and sometimes the difference is in where we turn our attention to. We can experience the same circumstances, yet have entirely different effects depending on whether we criticize what's happening or show compassion. We can find love in every interaction if we treat people and ourselves with respect and appreciation.

Dr. Robert A. Emmons, the world's leading scientific expert on gratitude, revealed that gratitude could help individuals struggling with depression and anxiety. It stimulates our brains to release serotonin and dopamine, some of the vital neurotransmitters responsible for the feeling of happiness. Gratitude practice could significantly reduce cardiac diseases, neurodegeneration, and inflammation. A regular gratitude ritual could help us build new neuropathways, rewiring ourselves to feel more positive throughout the day.[8]

When I interviewed Scott Schwenk, he shared that everything in life has a rhythm. If we want to change a circumstance, we have to see its rhythm, disrupt it, and create a new one. The experience of happiness has its rhythm as well, and gratitude can help strengthen it. Scott recommends having a few mindful moments throughout the day when you can

---

8   Madhuleena Roy Chowdhury, "The Neuroscience of Gratitude and How It Affects Anxiety & Grief," PositivePsychology, January 9, 2020.

touch some form of gratitude. It could be as simple as taking a few moments before every meal to give thanks for your health, for having a roof over your head, and for the food that fuels your body.

Visualization

Visualization is an exceptional practice that can help you attract what you want to have in your life, who you want to become, and how you want to feel. Many professional athletes and artists have used visualization techniques to get them closer to a successful outcome. Envisioning a victorious turn out of an event you may be worried about can help you build up confidence and reduce anxiety when the time to take action finally comes.

In 2019, I taught a workshop on creating a daily ritual, and I was quite nervous before the event. I rehearsed my talk in front of a mirror and recorded myself on camera, but it was still nothing like presenting in front of a live audience. I then decided to incorporate a visualization practice into my preparation. I imagined how I walked out to a group of friendly, genuinely engaged attendees who were interested in what I was sharing. In my visualization exercise, I was calm, and I smiled while presenting.

I imagined the room with a perfect temperature and that I felt calm, as if I was telling stories to my family and friends at a Christmas party. I also visualized that after the workshop, people came up to me and expressed how much they enjoyed the talk and how they looked forward to implementing some of the recommendations I shared.

Mentally rehearsing this scenario many times helped me build more confidence for the actual workshop, and when it was time for my presentation, I felt safe and welcomed. Of course, there were still moments when my heart was racing and my palms were sweaty, but I kept returning to my visualization, and it calmed me.

Whichever practices you pick to be part of your daily ritual, remember your *why*—why are you doing it, and what do you want to get out of it? Keep asking those questions until you hit gold and discover something that truly matters to you. Stay focused, commit to your ritual, and *fill your well with the water.* Performing your rituals with intention and dedication is the key. It will help you continue on your journey with grace and ease during challenging times.

CHAPTER EXERCISE:
CREATE YOUR DAILY RITUAL

When you begin to form your daily ritual, I invite you to exercise *the power of small steps.* Don't shoot for the stars right away. Start small but stay consistent. If you choose gratitude journaling as your daily ritual, start by writing down three simple things you are grateful for each day.

Based on my experience, rituals work best in the mornings and right before bed. For example, gratitude journaling in the morning can help you set the tone for the day. You can start by writing down something you are thankful for—a roof over your head, a cup of your favorite hot drink, or your fabulous body full of energy and vitality. Gratitude journaling at the end of the day can help you focus on all of the positive things that occurred throughout the day.

If you decide to take on meditation as your daily practice, start with just a few minutes a day and increase the duration as you develop consistency. Observing your breath during meditation can help you relax your busy mind. Start by sitting down in a comfortable position with your back straight. Inhale through your nose for a count of six, hold your breath for a count of four, and exhale through your mouth for a count of eight. By counting in your mind, you shift your attention away from everyday worries and into your body. Observe how you feel after meditation practice. If you notice more calmness in this state, start to gradually add more time to your practice. The point is to do it without straining yourself.

There are many exercises you can take on as your daily ritual. Regardless of your choice, I'd like to point out that the ritual is meant to serve you, not the other way around. If at some point you feel like you're doing it just because you committed to it, take a break and recalibrate. Don't do it to check the box. Remember your intention and *why* you're doing it.

CHAPTER 3:

HAPPY RELATIONSHIPS

———

"Love does not consist in gazing at each other, but in looking outward together in the same direction."

—ANTOINE DE SAINT-EXUPÉRY

Relationships are an essential part of our lives, right from the beginning to the very end. They can make or break us. At some point, we will experience blissful happiness and an overdose of love hormones. We are also likely to get our dreams crushed, and our pain and disappointment could make us wonder if it's worth opening up our hearts again.

Like many people, I've been in a situation where I've found what I thought was the perfect relationship. I celebrated, believing that I had met the partner who understood me and saw me the way I truly was; that I had a companion to share my life and to start a family. All of the astrological readings led me to that partnership, and it seemed that the Universe had a secret plan for just us two. And then we had our first argument, and the second one, and the third one. Our friends told us that it was normal, and that couples fought all the time. Time went by, and I started to notice characteristics of my partner that weren't there before. Or maybe they were, but I just didn't see them through my rose-colored glasses.

Unfortunately, this is the stage where many of us often make the mistake of trying to change, fix, or control our partners. If you've attended couples therapy or read books about relationships, you may remember that such behavior is a big no-no. Instead, we're supposed to love our partners unconditionally and accept them as they are. We set ourselves up for failure when we attach conditions to our love. *"I love you when you behave this way and because you do these things for me, but if you stop doing that, I won't love you so much anymore."* It's absolutely normal to want our partners to be better, but it's best if we don't attach our hopes to them changing, because that would mean setting expectations, and we all know where expectations get us!

Russell Brand, an English comedian and the host of the *Under the Skin* podcast, has opened up about the failures in his previous relationships and the core principles he applies in his current marriage. One of these principles is letting go of trying to control your partner. In one of his videos called "How to NOT Ruin a Relationship," Russell shared that by controlling our partners, criticizing their pursuits, and impeding on their friendships, we create a very unhealthy dynamic in a relationship.

We need to let go of unconsciously trying to groom them to meet our needs. Instead, we can give them the freedom to be their authentic selves and find ways to be more of service to them as partners. "Stay aware, and from that awareness, think, How can I be valuable? How can I be of service? What can I do for the person I'm in a relationship with?" said Russell.[9]

Not all situations are the same, so we have to apply this advice with reason and caution. What if your partner is physically, mentally, or emotionally abusive? Should you still practice unconditional love and ramp up your spiritual practice to get through it, or should you hold the boundary of your own wellbeing? Learning to accept and love your partner unconditionally is equally important in developing a healthy relationship as knowing your own boundaries and communicating them clearly. The wellbeing of both people in the relationship matters. If the other person is unwilling to respect your boundaries and continually violates them without accountability, then this is a sign that the relationship may be abusive.

There's always a chance that after using the tools offered in this chapter, there will still be friction in your relationship. You may give your partner all the freedom they need and support them on their journey, but if both of you are not compatible and cannot find a *frequency* for interacting, the relationship might fail. Perhaps the valuable lesson in this scenario would be recognizing the incompatibility early on and learning to walk away. A healthy relationship should be about multiplying the happiness between the two people,

---

9   Russell Brand, "How to NOT Ruin a Relationship," September 17, 2020, video, 9:59.

not getting sucked into one conflict after the next, thereby draining each other's energy.

Some couples love to fight. They argue, yell at each other, and break stuff, and then fifteen minutes later they have hot, passionate sex like nothing ever happened. Many individuals who grew up in homes where their parents yelled at each other are okay with such an environment. In fact, that's how they often seek attention. They would rather get yelled at than be ignored. For some of them, negative attention is better than no attention at all.

On the other hand, there are people who grew up in more peaceful environments that do not function well in heated arguments. Instead, they might shut down and go inward to process. Many of them solve challenges when they are calm, and they prefer the voice of reason instead of an emotional outburst. Even if you had a wonderful childhood, where your parents didn't yell and everything was *kumbaya* at your house, there might still be some *monsters hiding in your closet.*

Let Your Monsters Play Together

My spiritual teacher, Kai Karrel, a mystic and a shaman, has dedicated a significant part of his life to understanding relationships and helping couples develop healthy connections with each other. When I sat down to interview Kai, he shared a valuable teaching about our various traumas, or, as he likes to call them, our *inner monsters.* He said that monsters are not the actual problem. It's the fact that we hide them in the closet and refuse to engage with and understand them.

Kai invites us to open up to our partners and to discover that instead of rejecting us, they may actually accept us. In addition, seeing us opening up may allow them to do the same. They may even feel closer and more intimate with us, because now they have an opportunity to bring their monsters out as well, so that all of them can learn to get along.

"Let's assume that we have monsters that are conflicting. I have an anger monster, and you have a scared monster that freaks out and runs away when people yell at him. If we hide this from each other, we put ourselves at risk that there will be an explosion at a certain moment. Your angry monster will come out, scare mine, and I will run for the hills," shared Kai.

Instead of wasting months of our time hiding behind the facades of good girls and boys, Kai suggests that we have a monster chat very early on in our relationship. All it takes is sitting down with your partner and letting them know that one of your monsters is an angry monster. That you've studied it and you are friends, and you know that when it comes out, all it needs is a hug, or a cupcake, or whatever else it may want. In return, your partner can do the same and let you know how to handle their monster.

This way, when these monsters come to the surface next time, you won't be afraid of them because you'll remember how to manage them. You will be conscious of the fact that they come up because they're an integral part of what it means to be human. And if for some reason, you and the other person can't make peace with these monsters, you can find that out as early as possible. Thus, the time invested in a relationship is far shorter, and a break-up may be less devastating.

Unlike most authors who write about relationships, I don't have a successful marriage of thirty years with four kids and a dog. I was married for a year in my twenties, and since then I have had relationships with fantastic women, but none lasted longer than a few years. And believe me, I've tried. Together with my partners, I attended tantric seminars, couples therapy, energy healings, psychotherapy retreats, private sessions with spiritual teachers, ayahuasca ceremonies, traveled the world together, took cooking classes, salsa lessons, and read tons of relationship books. All of that was on top of the personal development work I did on my own.

That said, I have lots of experience in relationships that didn't work out, and since I'm the *glass half full* guy, I see every failed relationship as getting me closer to the successful one. I'm fortunate to have incredible teachers who help me extract valuable lessons from my relationships and apply them to my evolution, so I don't have to repeat the same mistakes over and over.

The Path of Desperation and the Path of Inspiration

In our recent interview, Kai Karrel shared that there are two ways to learn from a relationship—a path of desperation and inspiration. The desperation path happens at a point in our lives when we are saturated with pain from failed relationships and are tired of re-living the same scenario, only with different partners. It happens when, out of desperation, we are finally willing to change.

"Usually, desperation leads to recognition. Sit and journal about what did not work. It's not about what our partner did or did not do; it's about us. Where did we fail to express our boundaries? Where did we go against our core principles and jeopardize our inner truth?" said Kai. He emphasizes the importance of recognizing our failures, so that we can learn our lessons and move forward.

The inspiration path requires a slightly more proactive approach. Once you've acknowledged what didn't work and what could have been done differently in your previous relationships, you can begin to invite something new into your life. It's important to note that it's not about visualizing how your partner should look like or what hair color they must have. Kai suggests turning inward and instead envisioning how you want to feel and what kind of person you want to be in such a relationship.

"It should not be very different from who you are when you're by yourself. You should be fully expressed, with healthy boundaries, which brings us back to why self-love is so important. Because if I'm not happy with who I am, it's not going to change in a relationship. It's actually going to be worse. Your partner is going to be a mirror for you," shared Kai.

Taking Responsibility for Your Inner State

The biggest lesson I've learned over the years is that we are responsible for our inner states. We shouldn't blame others for the way we feel, and we shouldn't expect them to make us feel a certain way. If we are unhappy with ourselves, nobody in the world can change that but us. We have to figure this out on our own. Otherwise, we set up expectations for our relationships that ultimately cannot be met.

I used to tell my partner that her mood swings were hurting my writing flow and creativity. I expected her to become my muse and to inspire me to write. When that didn't happen, I blamed her for my lack of motivation. In reality, she had nothing to do with it. My writing and creativity were my responsibility. Sometimes it just didn't flow, but of course, I needed a reason. I needed to blame someone or something for lack of productivity, and more often than not, my partner was the easiest option.

Ironically, instead of taking responsibility for my inner state, I often took responsibility for my partner's inner state. Anytime she was in a poor mood, like a brave knight, I jumped in to rescue and cheer her up. It was my mission to make her happy and elevate her mood whenever she was down. Instead of holding space for those emotions I deemed unacceptable, I attempted to disrupt them as soon as possible, because it made *me* feel uncomfortable. Since the boundary between our inner states was compromised, I felt guilty about remaining in a pleasant mood if my partner was down, so I often found myself down in the trenches with her.

Dr. Brené Brown, a research professor at the University of Houston and *New York Times* best-selling author, has dedicated the past two decades studying vulnerability, courage, and empathy. In a beautifully animated video called "The

Power of Empathy" (with over sixteen million YouTube views), she shared her perspective on the difference between empathy and sympathy. "Empathy is a choice. And it's a vulnerable choice because, in order to connect with you, I have to connect with something in myself that knows that feeling," said Brené.[10]

In that video, she presents someone in a deep hole shouting that they are stuck and overwhelmed. Brené pointed out that an example of empathy would be to say that we've been in that hole, and we know what it's like to be there. We then would remind the person in the hole that they are not alone.

In the meantime, sympathy would be to attempt to cheer the person up and remind them of all the positive things in their life. "One of the things that we do sometimes, in the face of very difficult conversations, is we try to make things better. If I share something with you that's very difficult, I'd rather you say, 'I don't even know what to say right now. I'm just so glad you told me.' Because the truth is, rarely can a response make something better. What makes something better is a connection," shared Brené.

It's imperative to recognize we are not here to fix our partners or take away their pain. Pain carries valuable lessons and can be one of the most significant drivers for our personal growth. We should be more mindful of our attempts to shield our loved ones from the lessons they are supposed to learn. All we can do is firmly stand by their side, show compassion, and exercise non-judgment.

---

10   Brené Brown, "RSA Short: Empathy," December 10, 2013, video, 2:53.

Even though we may choose to be together for the rest of our lives, it's essential to leave some space for individual growth. In *The Prophet*, one of my favorite poets and philosophers, Kahlil Gibran, sums up a vision of an ideal relationship in the following way: "Let there be spaces in your togetherness, And let the winds of the heavens dance between you. Love one another but make not a bond of love: Let it rather be a moving sea between the shores of your souls. Fill each other's cup but drink not from one cup. Give one another of your bread but eat not from the same loaf. Sing and dance together and be joyous, but let each one of you be alone, even as the strings of a lute are alone though they quiver with the same music. Give your hearts, but not into each other's keeping. For only the hand of Life can contain your hearts. And stand together, yet not too near together: For the pillars of the temple stand apart, and the oak tree and the cypress grow not in each other's shadow."[11]

CHAPTER EXERCISE:
CORE PRINCIPALS FOR A HAPPY RELATIONSHIP

If you're choosing the path of inspiration, I invite you to start by setting up some core principles in your relationship. There's no need to reinvent the wheel, so I'll share with you the teaching I try to continually practice in my life. It comes from a renowned spiritual teacher and bestselling author—Don Miguel Ruiz. In his book, *The Four Agreements*, he shares the four principles that can lead us to experience

---

11   Kahlil Gibran, *The Prophet* (New York: Alfred A. Knopf, 1923), 15-16.

more happiness, freedom, and love.[12] Here is how you can apply these principles to create a healthy relationship with your partner. Keep in mind you don't need to take on all four agreements at once. Remember the power of small steps— celebrate consistent small victories. Implementing even just one of them can significantly transform your relationship.

Agreement number one: *Be impeccable with your word.* Words have a power to create and a power to destroy. So many relationships end because people say something they cannot take back. So if you find yourself in a heated conversation with your partner, for the sake of not saying something you may regret later, tell your partner that you need to take five minutes to collect your thoughts. Leave the room, breathe, return to your inner space, create security within yourself, and then return to the discussion. It is critically important to allow your partner this freedom as well. It can be hard to make space when things are heated, but there is no better time to step back and take a breath.

The second agreement suggests: *Don't take anything personally.* If you hear an accusation from your partner, don't assign a story to it and take it personally. Everyone is responsible for their own inner state. The best you can do in such a situation is to hold space, withhold judgment, and invite more compassion into your heart. When your partner blames you, try to remember that perhaps they are facing their inner monsters at this time and it has nothing to do with you.

---

12   Miguel Ruiz, *The Four Agreements: A Practical Guide to Personal Freedom* (San Rafael, CA: Amber-Allen Pub., 1997).

Don't make assumptions is the third agreement that may help you avoid miscommunications in your relationship. Instead of making up stories about your partner's inner state or feeling guilty about their mood, ask them a direct question: How are you feeling? Is there anything I can help you with? If your partner refuses to engage with you, return to agreement number two—*don't take anything personally.*

Finally, agreement number four: *Always do your best.* Don't be a perfectionist—your best and your partner's best may not look the same on the same day. Be mindful of where you are (your internal state) and which resources (time, energy—both physical and emotional) are available to you at the moment. One of my mentors often uses a metaphor that a taxi can take me anywhere I want, but first, I need to inform it of my location so it can come to get me. In other words, if you want to be at a point of mutual understanding with your partner but instead you're stuck with unresolved grudges, you need to acknowledge that first, release the grievances, and then take a step toward the desired destination.

CHAPTER 4:

FINDING FULFILLMENT AND HAPPINESS THROUGH WORK

———

"The two most important days in your life are the day you are born and the day you find out why."

—MARK TWAIN

From the time she was three years old, my friend, Kristin Brabant, was convinced she was put on this earth to become a teacher. Her mom, grandma, and aunt were all teachers. Her entire family had an alphabet soup of titles dribbling off the ends of their last names. A higher education degree meant security and prestige in the Brabant family. Naturally, growing up in such an environment, Kristin felt it was her calling to be an educator.

Kristin had been pursuing her master's degree in Effective Teaching when her health slowly started to decline. Various illnesses would overcome her body because she was holding on to a lot of stress. As soon as she healed one infection, another would arise in its place. Doctors could not figure out what was happening to her and kept prescribing various antibiotics.

Her inner guidance told her that this path was unsustainable. Kristin realized that the direction she was pursuing was not right for her and that she had to make a change. Every morning, she woke up with her stomach already in knots, dreading her day, with anxious thoughts flying through her mind: *You know this isn't right, Kristin. What are you going to do? You've invested your entire education and career in one skill, so what are you going to do if you quit?*

All of that mind chatter overwhelmed her, but Kristin told herself she was a fighter, not a quitter, and that she just needed to work harder. The fear of letting go of her identity as an educator paralyzed her; it kept her within her comfort zone, even though she was miserable.

Kristin is not the only person who had found herself in such a predicament. According to the Gallup World Poll, 85 percent of the world's one billion full-time workers are not engaged in their work. They are unhappy and stressed out.[13] For many of these individuals, their health deteriorates as a result of their work, and some don't even make it

---

13   Jim Harter, "Dismal Employee Engagement Is a Sign of Global Mismanagement," *Gallup*, 2021.

to retirement to enjoy the rest of their lives. On the other hand, some people love their jobs and don't even regard what they do as work; it's their way of living, their form of self-expression and identity.

Naturally, this leads me to wonder: Is our job just a way to acquire the means for survival, or could it be an instrument to positively impact numerous lives? How do we know if what we are doing is the right path for us?

We all want to be happy, but we sometimes compromise our happiness for a larger check or a more prestigious position. We can trick our minds into thinking the sacrifice is worth the reward, but our bodies know better. As soon as we engage in activities that deplete our life's energy, our bodies may send us a cautionary signal. In the beginning, these warnings can be as simple as a headache or digestive issues. Still, if we consistently disregard these signals, they can eventually evolve into a major situation where we may be forced to completely stop until we change course.

When Kristin's deteriorating health forced her to fully stop, she left her master's program. As soon as she made this decision, she felt liberated. She was scared, but free. This freedom was a new feeling for her, and it took some time to adjust. Kristin had long associated success with stress, and now was her chance to redefine that connection. She often felt guilty about her freedom, as if she had taken the easy route. Nevertheless, Kristin knew she had made the correct choice because her health quickly started to improve. Within a short time, her various illnesses went away, and she was back on her feet.

Her turning point was realizing that she wasn't created to be miserable. Kristin knew that challenges were essential for growth, but she realized her misery went beyond that. As she told me in our *Think Clever* podcast interview, "I finally accepted it. I love myself! I showed myself that I'm valuable and worthy by letting go of what no longer served me. I trusted that my next steps would be revealed to me, but I had to take a leap before I saw the net."

Follow Your Excitement

The biggest thing that helped Kristin identify her next step was paying attention to what lit her up. She penned the experiences that gave her energy and aligned with her path, and the ones that drained that energy and made her feel more disconnected and lost. "We're always investing energy in something. Certain things, people, and activities return this energy to us manifold. And then there are the ones that suck the life out of us," shared Kristin.

Kristin realized that even though she didn't want to be a school instructor, she still appreciated the process of teaching. She enjoyed helping people uncover their strengths and use them to achieve their goals in life. Following her excitement led her to new opportunities and jobs where she could further develop this skill. Kristin didn't know where she would end up, but she focused on making sure she kept moving in a direction that lit her up more than the previous step she had taken.

"If you follow what lights you up, and you dare to go and tell people that this is what you intend to create, then you are opening yourself up to receive the guidance, the support, and the unexpected helpers on your path. They will get you closer and closer to living out your mission in its fullest expression," said Kristin.

Eventually, Kristin's pursuit of the excitement led her to her dream job as a success coach for female entrepreneurs. Every day, she helps inspiring women achieve their biggest professional and personal goals with greater ease and enjoyment. Her tools, workshops, and business coaching have already helped thousands of women lead more fulfilling, impactful, and vibrant businesses. Most importantly, Kristin is healthy, and she loves what she gets to do every day.

I'm convinced that the Universe has a unique path for each one of us and that when we are off track, it gives us gentle nudges to get us back into alignment. The gentleness of such nudges depends on how comfortable we are within our suffering and how afraid we are to take the leap of faith. Perhaps when we complete a chapter of our lives and learn the assigned lesson, we're supposed to move on to keep growing and evolving. However, if we ignore the nudges and decide to stay within our comfort zone, our growth stagnates, and we get stuck in our regular ruts.

In 2018, I participated in a retreat with one of my favorite spiritual teachers, Eckhart Tolle, and he said something to our group that I continually revisit. He told us that suffering was necessary only until we realized that it was unnecessary. He added that once we get to a point where we've had enough of it, we'll be able to say that we don't need it anymore.

Suffering serves a purpose. It drives us to seek the truth and to come into alignment with our unique design. It's not necessarily the most pleasant method for inspiring change, but it's really up to us how much of it we choose to endure. "Some people awaken spiritually without ever coming into contact with any meditation technique or any spiritual teaching. They may awaken simply because they can't stand the suffering anymore," said Tolle in his book, *Stillness Speaks.*[14]

I resonate with Kristin's story because I was once on a very similar path. When I graduated from college, my first job was as a financial advisor. That career path satisfied my ambitions, I had great camaraderie with my colleagues, and I felt important when I would dress in a suit and tie every morning. Being a financial advisor required me to repeatedly get out of my comfort zone and look for new clients. Even though it was challenging, I was in my twenties and I had lots to prove to myself, my parents, and my friends.

My sense of fulfillment from this job dissipated after the second year, but I stayed with the company for almost two more years. Like my friend Kristin, I kept telling myself I was not a quitter and pushed even harder. Regardless of how strenuously I worked, things were no longer flowing for me. It became more challenging to obtain new clients, and many of my deals started to fall apart. Deep inside, I knew I did not have any passion for the financial industry and that it didn't excite me anymore. Quite frankly, I didn't have a clue what excited me at that time. I tried brainstorming exercises and various tests to help narrow down my interests and point

---

14   Eckhart Tolle, *Stillness Speaks* (Novato, CA: New World Library, 2003).

me in the right direction, but I was met with nothing but dead silence.

I buckled down and kept grinding, only this time with feelings of despair and hopelessness. Since my job no longer excited me, I tried finding excitement elsewhere and often ended up looking for it in bars and nightclubs. I did whatever I could to distract myself from the fact that my work no longer fulfilled me.

After about four years, I finally realized that my lifestyle had become unhealthy. I felt that if I didn't transition into something else soon, I would face significant health issues. Shortly after, I was presented with an opportunity to take over a Ukrainian swimwear brand and expand it in the United States. Becoming an entrepreneur and running my own business sounded amazing, so I jumped on board with this proposition. Once again, I made this decision based on how the job would look to my friends and family, instead of following what excited me.

Fortunately, this time it didn't take me four years to realize I was living somebody else's dream again. Things escalated very quickly because the pressure was on from day one, and it showed up in many ways. Since I was working from home, there wasn't any separation between my personal life and my work; I was always at the office. There were many arguments between my business partners and myself because we couldn't agree on the company's vision.

After spending a year in such a toxic environment, my health started to deteriorate. I was perpetually on edge and was not the positive and outgoing guy I used to be. Within a short time, I had two nervous breakdowns and realized it was time to recalibrate my entire inner world. I understood that I needed to stop trying to fit into someone I was not. Like Kristin, I finally decided to take the road less traveled and follow my heart. I stopped everything I was doing, got a one-way ticket to Southeast Asia, and went on a journey of self-discovery, which you will learn more about later in this book.

Find Your Uniqueness

I have a reason to believe there is an optimal path that lets us experience a sense of fulfillment and joy from our work while bringing the most value to the people around us. Deep inside, we are all artists with distinct talents that define our unique perspectives, and it's our duty to discover that within us and share it with the rest of the world. Sadly, many people are hesitant to explore their uniqueness through their work. They settle for stability, comfort, and security instead of taking the road less traveled. And that's okay. It's impossible to have 7.8 billion unique careers. Yet we can each express ourselves differently even within the same profession.

My friend, Jen Jones, is an American architect of thirty years. She found an exciting niche within the architecture industry by following her inner guidance and connecting her passion for architecture with her enthusiasm for spiritual growth. When Jen was eight years old, she had started developing seizures. She was a very sensitive child and got overwhelmed easily. Right before the seizures would happen, Jen would experience a profound awakening of sharpened sounds and a heightened sense of smell. Then, the seizure would happen. This happened for many years, and Jen slowly started managing it through lifestyle changes. She had her very last episode when she was in her twenties during an architecture school trip to Venice, Italy.

At that time, Jen was in a program where they studied various monasteries throughout Europe. Together with her class, she was visiting one of the sacred sites when suddenly her senses became heightened. Jen started seeing lights and hearing sounds that no one else was able to perceive. She began to fall forward, her spine became erect, and she fell straight down, hitting her head on the cobblestone floor.

"I was fully awake and observed myself in my body. I saw people running toward me. When I came back into my body, I knew that I had seen a realm of subtle energy and experienced a different type of consciousness," Jen shared in our interview. This occurrence sparked her curiosity and inspired her to better understand her out-of-body experience.

When she returned to the United States, Jen started working with a spiritual healer to understand the world of subtle energy. She also signed up for yoga classes to better connect with her body. During her fifth year of architecture school, Jen started studying indigenous and tribal cultures and decided to write her thesis on the Anasazi and their primal space concepts.

Jen spent the next twenty-five years merging architecture with her spiritual path. She found more ways in which these two practices intertwined. Her journey of curiosity and inspiration led her to become one of the few Vaastu architects authorized to practice in Vishwakarma's lineage. Her work enables her to incorporate an ancient Indian approach to architecture that focuses on subtle energies for well-being, peace, and abundance.[15]

There are different ways to learn life's lessons on your journey of self-discovery. You can learn from suffering, or you can take the path of inspiration and learn by following what excites you. Both ways are equally valuable. There is no right or wrong path, but after spending a substantial portion of my life learning through suffering, I can say that the inspiration route is a lot more fun. All it takes is learning to become more in tune with your body and recognizing the signals that it sends whenever you approach a situation that can be potentially harmful or beneficial for you.

CHAPTER EXERCISE:
WHERE DO YOU INVEST YOUR ENERGY?

It's time for some introspection! Turn your journal to a new page and make three columns. In the first column, list everything that you like about your job. Perhaps you enjoy the company of the people you work with or that it provides financial security for you, or maybe it has the best coffee and snacks in the break room. Add as many things you can think of into this part.

In the second column, note everything you dislike about your job: long commute, unappreciative management, stagnation

---

15   Jen Jones, "Vasstu Architecture: An Ancient Approach for Modern Times," *Jen Jones Architecture*, March 2, 2019.

of your career growth, or energy-draining clients—something that you think about over and over and complain about to your friends. Finally, the last column is your exploration, where you can list all of your hobbies or something new you've always wanted to try. Now that you have a pretty clear overview of your job, you can create a solid plan.

First, look at the second column where you listed everything you dislike about your work and create a game plan to reduce the emotional charge those items carry or even eliminate them altogether. My experience from previous jobs and even while writing this book has taught me that if we don't address something that bothers us, we'll keep leaking energy until we finally take care of it.

Let's say you have a coworker who continually crosses your boundaries, and they are not even aware of it. It frustrates you to the point that you even consider switching jobs, but instead of facing them, you sweep it under a rug and let the frustration build up. If you leave it unattended, you'll keep wasting your energy thinking and complaining about this situation over and over. Instead, I invite you to create a plan on how to resolve this so you can focus on everything that excites you about your work.

This exercise can also take you into another direction. Add items from your hobbies column and mix them with things that frustrate you about your job. For example, you may be unable to eliminate the long commute to work, but you can combine it with something exciting, so it doesn't feel dreadful—you can listen to audiobooks or learn a new language while driving to work and back home.

One of the items on my dislike list is that I'm averse to sitting in front of my laptop for many hours in a row. Something that I have on my list of hobbies is that I am committed to doing one hundred pushups each day. When I mix those two together, I create a win-win situation. I get to take more breaks between my work while fulfilling my commitment on daily pushups and maintaining a good physical shape. It's not going to be this easy with each item on your dislike list, but it can help you address whatever is within your reach at the moment.

CHAPTER 5:

THE ABUNDANCE MINDSET

———

"If you look at what you have in your life, you'll always have more. If you look at what you don't have in life, you'll never have enough."

—OPRAH WINFREY

For most of us, the process of awakening to a more conscious way of living is filled with many revelations and insights. They may seem like insignificant events to others, but to us as individuals, they have the power to shift our entire perception of the world. Sometimes it's a simple act of kindness that inspires us to change our lives for the better or a moment when we come close to something important to us that gets us out of our comfort zones. It's a moment that shifts our viewpoint and makes us assess our lives differently. In these instances, we let go of the fear that had been holding us back, and we encounter a new sense of freedom that helps us experience life from a different perspective.

Anthony Robbins, a world-renowned motivational speaker, author, and philanthropist, shared one of such moments that helped him start experiencing life from a different perspective. It happened when he was still a young man and was struggling financially to stay afloat. He was down to his last $20 and didn't know what to do next. Amid his frustration, he decided to go eat at an all-you-can-eat salad bar three miles from his home.

Once he got there, he ate everything he could possibly eat. While he was dining, the door opened, and a beautiful woman walked in. Tony waited to see who she was with, but there wasn't a boyfriend or a husband; there was just a boy dressed in a suit. He held the door for his mom, pulled out the chair, and sat her down. The young lad was such a gentleman that it truly moved Tony.

When Tony paid his bill, he still had about $15 left. On his way out, he approached the little boy, said hello, and shook his hand. Tony told him that he saw how he opened the lady's door and what a gentleman he was. The boy got shy and said that the lady was his mom. "Even better," said Tony. "It's so cool you're taking her to lunch like this."

The boy said he wasn't taking her to lunch since he was only eleven years old and he didn't have a job yet. At that moment, Tony reached into his pocket and put all of the money he had on a table, exclaiming, "Yes, you are taking her to lunch!" He shook the boy's hand and walked out of the restaurant.

"As I exited the restaurant, I felt purely euphoric at the moment when I should have been the most freaked out. I just gave away my last dollar! But I had zero fears. I've heard of people going on a fast and surviving without food, so I was ready to do the same. I felt positive about it," said Tony Robbins in his podcast interview with Lewis Howes.[16]

That day, Tony Robbins became a wealthy man. He realized that his sense of security was not attached to these last fifteen bucks. When he walked out of that restaurant, he had zero dollars in his pocket, yet he felt optimistic. Tony traded his scarcity mindset for one of abundance and released his fears of not having enough. He made a conscious psychological, emotional, and spiritual shift that altered the course of his life.

The Scarcity Mindset

The scarcity mindset keeps us encumbered by fear that we don't have enough. We are afraid that we have insufficient time, money, love, or fill in the blank. A feeling of lack of security often accompanies this type of limiting thinking. Not only do we believe we lack the resources to exist, we fear we may lose what we've already secured. Scarcity thinking proliferates a fear that there are limited resources and we must compete with each other. Instead of getting together to cocreate something new, many people choose to compete for what's already out there.

---

16   Tony Robbins, "7 Simple Steps to Master the Game of Money with Tony Robbins (Episode 109)," interview by Lewis Howes, in *School of Greatness*, November 25, 2014, podcast, audio, 52:44.

The scarcity mindset created slogans like *"the early bird gets the worm"* to motivate us to keep moving without taking a break to consider whether our achievements make us any happier. I believe Mark Twain's response to this slogan is the best I've seen—"Rise early. It is the early bird that catches the worm. Don't be fooled by this absurd law; I once knew a man who tried it. He got up at sunrise and a horse bit him."[17]

We set ourselves up for failure when we attach our sense of security to ephemeral things. Like many people, I was afraid I didn't have enough. I was determined to change that by accumulating things I thought provided me a sense of security and stability. I believed that once I got a bigger apartment, I would feel more secure. Or, once I got a different job, I would become more stable. I bought nice clothes, joined elite gyms, and dined at expensive restaurants. I strived to move up in the world to feel more established. As I approached my vision of what made me feel safe, something shattered my false sense of security. In March 2020, I traveled for ten days to Portugal. As my travels were coming to an end, coronavirus struck, and most of the world went into lockdown.

For various reasons, I spent the next twelve months living out of a suitcase. I gave up my apartment, the fortress that was keeping me safe. My friends returned my brand new car to the dealership. I gave away my furniture and most of my clothes. Whatever was left from the fourteen years of living

---

17 "Rise early. It is the early bird that catches the worm. Don't be fooled by this absurd law; I once knew a man who tried it. He got up at sunrise and a horse bit him," Mark Twain Quotations - Early Rising, accessed April 29, 2021.

in Los Angeles fit into a five-by-fix storage space. Within a matter of a few months, the possessions I had acquired that gave me a sense of security and stability were gone, yet I was okay. I actually felt freer than ever before. I recognized that I didn't need any of those things to feel safe in this world. I realized that I already had everything I needed to live a comfortable life.

The Abundance Mindset

An abundance mindset takes a very different perspective on your reality. It allows you to give without expecting to receive anything in return. Instead of competing for limited resources, you create resources. It's a total shift of mindset from competition to co-creation. When you adopt an abundance mentality, you align with like-minded individuals to generate more value for everyone around. You are not afraid that somebody may steal your idea and make a billion dollars with it because you believe there's a lot more where it came from.

My friend Al Tutson, the founder of TIGER Success Inc., an organization that helps people unlock their potential to experience life at its ultimate, lives by the advice he gives to his clients. His childhood involved many obstacles, but he did not allow that to deter him from thinking he had everything he needed to achieve his dreams. While acknowledging his life was a lot more challenging than it was for many of his peers, he did not allow the scarcity thinking to plant the seeds of fear in his mind.

Al stayed very conscious of any negative self-talk and cut it off as soon as it started dragging him into feeling that he didn't have enough. He trained himself to see abundance everywhere he looked and saw opportunities to learn where others saw only failures. Al followed his credo, "The only power you have over me is the power I give you." He trained himself to apply less judgment to situations. Instead of labeling them good or bad, he exercised patience because, as it often happens in life, some of the experiences that seem unfortunate at first very often turn out to be a blessing in disguise.

When I interviewed Al, he shared that ultimately everyone gets their reward. Some people get it sooner, while others may have to work a little harder to get it. It really depends on what this reward represents to us. To some individuals, it means spending plenty of time with their family and being at home to raise their kids. To others, it may be climbing up the career ladder and securing their financial freedom. Success in life looks different for each person. Once you recognize what it looks like for you, you only need to worry about moving toward your dream. There's no need to worry about how success looks to other people and how they plan on getting there.

Wallace D. Wattles, the author of an all-time classic on wealth creation, *The Science of Getting Rich,* wrote, "Man can form things in his thought, and by impressing his thought upon formless substance can cause the thing he thinks about to be created. In order to do this, man must pass from the competitive to the creative mind; otherwise, he cannot be in harmony with the Formless Intelligence, which is always creative and never competitive in spirit."[18]

Formless Intelligence, the Universe, God, Great Spirit, or Gaia all refer to a higher power through which things come into existence. Being in harmony and tapping into your creativity allows you to co-create with others and the Universe. That state is only possible when you're not living in fear that you may run out of ideas, food, or time. Co-creation with the Universe becomes available to you when you remain in a state of abundance.

Wattles further guides us into the universal principles by sharing yet another vital element in the process of co-creation. He says the way to come into harmony with the Formless Substance is through a sincere gratitude practice for everything you have in your life. "Gratitude unifies the mind of man with the intelligence of Substance, so that man's thoughts are received by the Formless. Man can remain upon the creative plane only by uniting himself with the Formless Intelligence through a deep and continuous feeling of Gratitude," Wattles writes.

Gratitude Is a Doorway to Abundance

My entry point into the abundance mindset was through a daily gratitude practice. I used the *where attention goes, energy flows* principle we discussed in the first chapter to shift my attention away from the things I didn't have and instead

---

18   Wallace D. Wattles, *The Science of Getting Rich: How to Make Money and Get the Life You Want* (Scotts Valley: CreateSpace, 2015).

focus on what was already available to me. I did it by keeping a daily gratitude journal for an entire year.

Every morning I woke up and wrote down three things I was grateful for in my life—my health, family, friends, travels, teachers, anything I could think of that brought positive feelings into my life. Then right before bed, I wrote down three things I was thankful for that happened that day. Even on the lousy days, I found at least three things I appreciated.

I wrote in this gratitude journal for 365 days, and after an entire year, I had 2,190 items I was grateful for. Indeed, some things repeated once in a while, but there were lots of new items as well. Imagine, how do you think you would feel if you had so much to be grateful for? Do you think you'd still struggle with feeling you don't have enough? It's important to point out that it wouldn't be as powerful of practice to just list all of those items all at once on the first day. The key is to train our minds to look for experiences to be thankful for on a daily basis.

These days my gratitude practice consists of saying a prayer before every meal to give thanks for everything I have in my life. Doing this as a regular practice helps me to stay in the abundance mindset. Daily gratitude practice helped me realize how much I already had. It also helped me clarify what I wanted to attract into my life and what I no longer needed in my life.

CHAPTER EXERCISE:
FOCUSED GRATITUDE

One of the simplest ways to form an abundance mindset is to start giving thanks for everything you already have. However, this practice can become even more effective if you first focus on the areas in your life where you still believe you don't have enough.

Reflect in your journal on where the scarcity mindset still prevails in your life. Write anything you can think of and be as detailed as possible.

Next, write everything that you already have in those same areas where you still feel lack. List anything that comes to mind regardless of how insignificant it may seem at first. Notice what catches your attention. Is there something on this list that you take for granted and stopped appreciating? Are there elements that seem insignificant in comparison to what others already have? Can you see their value and appreciate them more when you look at them without judging or comparing?

When I recently did this exercise, I realized that one of the areas where I believed I still had lack was my *Think Clever* podcast. When I compared my show to the ones of Aubrey Marcus or Tim Ferris, I felt I didn't have many listeners, and therefore my podcast wasn't bringing much value to anyone. However, when I did the second part of this exercise, I realized that hundreds of people were already listening to each episode that I released. I imagined how a hundred people would look like in a room, and I realized how much I appreciated that. What once was an area I complained about became my space of gratitude.

For the next twenty-one days, I invite you to focus on recognizing and appreciating the elements that stood out to you the most in the second part of this exercise. Consider including them in your gratitude practice as often as possible, and open up to a possibility that an area of your life where you encountered scarcity may become your place of abundance.

CHAPTER 6:

HAPPINESS IS IN YOUR GUT

———

"To keep the body in good health is a duty... otherwise we shall not be able to keep the mind strong and clear."

—BUDDHA

In the fall of 2017, I started experiencing issues with my digestion. In the beginning, it was just discomfort and bloating, but it worsened as time went on. I thought I had a pretty healthy lifestyle, but just in case, I included more veggies into my diet. Unfortunately, it didn't help, and instead, it got to a point where my belly was so bloated it looked as if I was pregnant. I finally went to a hospital where they ran lots of different tests on me, but not much came up. One of the doctors concluded that I probably had some bacteria in my gut and needed to take antibiotics to kill it.

I followed his recommendation, but my condition didn't get any better. It actually got worse. As I later discovered, antibiotics kill all bacteria—good and bad. We need good bacteria to cultivate a proper gut flora and prevent disease. According to a recent research study published in the Chinese Medical Journal: "A growing number of studies have shown that antibiotics can result in microbial dysbiosis, and the disruption of gut microbiota in neonates and adults contributes to numerous diseases, including diabetes, obesity, inflammatory bowel disease, asthma, rheumatoid arthritis, depression, autism, and superinfection in critically ill patients."[19]

I started experiencing mood swings, fatigue, panic attacks, and social anxiety. It got to the point that I was afraid to step out of my apartment, and I couldn't be in crowded places, even with my friends. Things escalated very quickly, and I decided to see a doctor again, but this time he advised me to start taking anti-depressants. Once again, I followed his advice, but now I suspected that my body was telling me that it was time for me to take a more holistic approach with my health.

The Answer Is on Our Plates

Stressful jobs, failed relationships, and unfulfilled dreams can indeed become sources of unhappiness. Yet, the answer is quite often right in front of us—it's in our food. Many people don't get enough essential nutrients needed to maintain a

19   Sheng Zhang and De-Chang Chen, "Facing a New Challenge: The Adverse Effects of Antibiotics on Gut Microbiota and Host Immunity," *Chinese Medical Journal* 132, no. 10 (May 20, 2019): 1135-1138.

healthy lifestyle. They also lack nutritional literacy to make better choices when it comes to food. You see, not all food is the same for each person. As the popular idiom goes, "one man's food is another man's poison." Human beings are very complex and unique.

Just because spinach is trending and the entire world is eating it, it doesn't mean that it's suitable for everyone. We need to have a specific type of bacteria to help digest certain types of foods. So even if spinach had the most nutrients from all the other plants, still, if your gut has difficulties digesting it, this wholesome vegetable can sit in your digestive tract for a long time. Your body can use up a lot of energy trying to digest it, making it a lot less beneficial for you and most likely harmful.

The kind of food we eat matters, or else we wouldn't see all the health issues related to a poor diet. Some food types can cause so much inflammation in your gut that you will be irritated and stressed out throughout the day regardless of how much you meditate. Many of us don't realize that most of the serotonin, our happiness hormone, is produced in the gut. If that happens to be our problem area, mood swings, anxiety, and even depression can become expected consequences.[20] You may be eating something that produces inflammation in your body and causes it to redirect its energy to continually repair itself. In that case, you may not have much energy left for other activities in your day. Ultimately, you are running

---

20   Duo-Chen Jin et al. "Regulation of the serotonin transporter in the pathogenesis of irritable bowel syndrome," *World Journal of Gastroenterology* vol. 22,36 (2016): 8137-48.

on an empty tank, fighting a battle you may not even be aware of.

When I got the nudge from my body that it was time to become more proactive with my health, I began to read lots of articles and books about the relationship between mental health and gut health. The more I researched, the more I realized how much of a connection these two areas had. I attended various wellness summits and learned a lot in the process. I recognized that the wellness field fascinated me and that I had the tools to improve my health so I wouldn't have to depend on medications for the rest of my life.

I signed up for a twelve-month course with the Institute for Integrative Nutrition (IIN) to become an integrative nutrition health coach. Initially, my goal was to learn more about my own health and how to strengthen it. I didn't start out intending to become a health coach to work with other people, but I learned so much in the process of my education that I just naturally started sharing with others. Halfway through the IIN curriculum, I discovered gut microbiome testing and its ability to show which foods are good for us and which ones we should stay away from. Surprisingly, many vegetables I added to my diet while attempting to heal my digestion were in the red zone for me.

At the time, the test I did was with Viome, a company specializing in personalized food recommendations based on your microbiome analysis. It showed that my gut flora was not suitable for vegetables like bell peppers, cucumbers, and tomatoes. Precisely the core ingredients of the salads I ate daily. Instead of fueling my body with the necessary nutrients from the greens, it turned out that I created the perfect environment for inflammation of my gastrointestinal region.

Is Inflammation the Cornerstone of Our Problems?

Dr. David Perlmutter, a board-certified neurologist and a five-time *New York Times* bestselling author, focuses on brain health through a nutritional approach. In his book, *The Grain Brain*, he explains the effect inflammation has on our bodies: "Inflammation, which you know by now is the cornerstone of many brain disorders, can be initiated when the immune system reacts to a substance in a person's body. When antibodies of the immune system come into contact with a protein or antigen to which a person is allergic, the inflammatory cascade is provoked, releasing a whole host of damaging chemicals known as cytokines."[21] He shared that inflammation helps our bodies combat infection and recover from injuries, but it becomes a significant problem when it stays for an extended time and can cause various chronic degenerative conditions.

If you twist your ankle, your body will respond by sending immune cells and various proteins to the injury site so it can start the repair process. Your ankle will most likely swell up due to the inflammation, but it will go back to normal when the healing is complete. That's the proper role inflammation

---

21   David Perlmutter and Kristin Loberg, *Grain Brain: The Surprising Truth about Wheat, Carbs, and Sugar — Your Brain's Silent Killers* (London: Yellow Kite, 2019).

serves in our bodies. However, if you have inflammation in your gut but it doesn't have visible symptoms, you may never find out about it until you go and run some tests. You may be walking around tired, struggling with brain fog, and trying to fix the problem with a cup of coffee or an energy drink instead of examining the contents of your plate.

When I completed my gut microbiome test and got my results back, it showed that most of the grains I consumed daily were on the "avoid list" for me. This news opened up a whole new can of worms. I learned that most common grains like wheat, corn, and rice are major contributors to inflammation for many people worldwide. Max Lugavere, a filmmaker, health journalist, and a *New York Times* best-selling author, educates people about the severe consequences of consuming these grains.

In his talk "Dementia Is Preventable Through Lifestyle. Start Now," Max said, "The most insidious thing about these three grains is that today they're pulverized, and packaged, and sold to us in processed foods that line our supermarket aisles. These ultra-processed foods now make up 60 percent of the calories that we consume worldwide." He went on to add that when we consume these exact kinds of foods, they set off the equivalent of a forest fire in our bodies, and our brains sit directly downwind of that fire. "That fire that I'm talking about is called inflammation, and inflammation directly accelerates brain aging," said Max.[22]

---

22   Max Lugavere, "Dementia Is Preventable Through Lifestyle," filmed November 2, 2018 in Venice Beach, CA, TEDx video, 19:37.

When I interviewed my friend, Conni Biesalski, an author, filmmaker, and host of the *CREATE* podcast show, she shared about the role gut health played in her life. Conni revealed that at the end of 2017, she hit a low point in her life. Her gut issues were getting worse, she was experiencing a lot of anxiety, and she was on an emotional roller coaster. Conni was in the process of creating more content, but because of the continuous struggle with brain fog, she kept hitting the creator's block.

She was living in Bali, Indonesia, at the time, and a new acquittance turned out to be a godsend for her. "I moved into a new house in Bali, and a couple of months later, we got a new housemate, and she was a naturopathic doctor who specialized in gut health. So, the Universe sent me the right person, right into my house," said Conni.

When she shared with her new roommate, Kirsten, what she was going through, Kirsten said that everything pointed in the direction of a small intestinal bacterial overgrowth (SIBO). Conni's new naturopathic roommate told her that many people actually have this condition and are not even aware of it. She informed her that bloating had become so common that many people think it's a normal part of the digestive process. However, the problem is not just about the discomfort and degeneration caused by inflammation, rather the fact that it inhibits our gut's ability to produce serotonin—a hormone essential to our ability to experience happiness.

Luckily for Conni, her diet contained the answer to her problems. Kirsten explained that eating foods that created a low-grade inflammation was the cause of Conni's suffering. "I switched to an anti-inflammatory diet and had to eliminate all of the gluten, sugar, alcohol, and caffeine—anything that fed the bacteria and created inflammation within my body. I also had to give up all the bread and cookies, because those are carbohydrates, and they convert into sugar as well," shared Conni.

Once Conni understood the connection between her diet and her overall well-being, it got a lot easier to make better meal choices. Eliminating foods she was used to was not an easy process. It was a complete makeover of her lifestyle, but these changes allowed her to be the healthy and happy person she is today. She got rid of the brain fog and fatigue and finished writing her book, *Find Your Magic*.

The Gut-Brain Connection

Something that many people are not aware of is that our gut is our second brain. Scientists call it the enteric nervous system (ENS), and it is connected to our central nervous system (CNS), which is how these two brains communicate with each other. Whenever we experience irritation in the gastrointestinal system, a signal is sent out to CNS, triggering mood change. "For decades, researchers and doctors thought that anxiety and depression contributed to these problems. But our studies and others show that it may also be the other way around," explained Jay Pasricha, MD director of the Johns Hopkins Center for Neurogastroenterology, whose research and publications on the enteric nervous and gut-brain axis has gathered attention around the world.[23]

Some research studies have gone to the extent of discovering a connection between our gut microbiome and our personality traits. Evidently, having more diverse bacteria in your gut supports your mood and makes you more social, creating more robust networks. Dr. Katerina Johnson from the Department of Psychology at Oxford University focuses her research on the relationship between the microbiome and behavioral traits. In her recent study, she shared, "This is the first study to find a link between sociability and microbiome diversity in humans and follows on from similar findings in primates which have shown that social interactions can promote gut microbiome diversity. This result suggests the same may also be true in human populations."[24]

When I created a blueprint for my health, I got a clear picture of which foods promoted my well-being and gave me energy and which ones drained that energy out of me. This process was not a quick transformation but an entire lifestyle adjustment. I had to change the behavioral patterns I had since I was a kid. Looking back at it, I can sincerely say that it was well worth it. In the beginning, I had to eliminate anything that could possibly cause inflammation in my body—sugar, caffeine, alcohol, wheat, dairy, and a few other foods. I took a

---

23   Atsushi Kamiya, MD, "The Brain-Gut Connection," *Johns Hopkins Medicine: Health*, accessed February 18, 2021.

24   Katerina V.A. Johnson, "Gut Microbiome Composition and Diversity Are Related to Human Personality Traits," *Human Microbiome Journal* 15 (March 2020): 1-15.

long break from consuming those foods and saw tremendous improvements in my health.

My gut inflammation went down, my mood swings stabilized, and I had more energy throughout the day. Most importantly, I had a much more optimistic view on my life. Today, I drink coffee with a pastry once in a while, and I can have a few glasses of wine. But I'm more conscious about my choices, and I approach it as a treat, not as a regular part of my diet. I have eliminated most of the junk food, including sodas, from my life. These days, I pay more attention to where my food comes from. As soon as I feel a little off, I take a break and allow my body to restore itself to normal. Food is a powerful instrument that can become a cure or a toxin. It's our responsibility to become educated about our choices.

The most important thing I learned from my healing journey is this idea of bio-individuality—what's good for one person may not be so suitable for another one. It's imperative to discover your individual blueprint for everything in life—your own recipe for happiness, fulfillment, relationships, and nutrition. The intention of this chapter is not to replace the advice of a medical professional, but rather inspire you to learn more about your own health and stop taking it for granted. The sooner you understand what's right for your body and what you should stay away from, the better quality of life you can start living. Your body is a self-healing machine, but it needs proper nutrients to conduct the repair process.

CHAPTER EXERCISE:
TAKE INVENTORY OF YOUR EATING HABITS

On a scale of one to ten, how satisfied are you with your diet? Do you find a correlation between eating certain foods and a shift in your energy levels or your overall mood? People are creatures of habit. We can get used to many conditions, even if they are quite unhealthy for us. But if we don't pay attention, things may go unnoticed, and eventually, we may find ourselves stuck with unhealthy eating habits. Becoming conscious of what you eat can be the best mindfulness practice.

This is your opportunity to take inventory of your eating habits, especially the unhealthy ones. It's one thing to be aware of them somewhere deep inside, and it's a whole different story when you list all of them on a piece of paper and stare at them. So I invite you to take your journal out and answer the following questions:

- Do you eat when you're stressed? What are the things that most often provoke stress eating for you?
- Do you eat junk food? Which guilty pleasures do you usually turn to?
- Are you dependent on coffee to get through the day? Are you hydrating properly?
- How many times a week do you eat less than two hours before bedtime?
- Do you get sleepy right after lunch and find it difficult to maintain focus and productivity?
- Do you experience discomfort with your digestion throughout the day? If yes, does that happen after you consume a specific type of food?

- Which types of foods do you feel you should eliminate from your diet?

Now that you have a better picture of your eating habits, look for connections. What do you think needs to change in your lifestyle? If overall you're quite satisfied with your diet, but you feel like you could take a break from a particular guilty pleasure (coffee, alcohol, sweets) or a lifestyle habit (watching TV while eating dinner, snacking while you're stressed out, eating late) it may be a good idea to get an accountability partner. If you feel ready to make a more drastic change, I recommend working with a professional. There are many amazing naturopathic doctors, nutritionists, and health coaches who can help you reach your goals.

CHAPTER 7:

MIND TRAINING

———

"Happiness can be achieved
through training the mind."

—HIS HOLINESS THE DALAI LAMA

Do you ever find yourself in a situation where you are driving but you don't even remember getting into the car? Or when you finish your lunch in ten minutes without ever registering the taste of your food because you're distracted by reading the news or watching funny videos on YouTube? These are just a few examples of how many of us operate on autopilot, mindlessly conducting the same activities again and again.

Dr. Joe Dispenza, one of the most well-known experts on mind training, explores the consequences of conducting our lives on autopilot in his book, *Evolve Your Brain: The Science of Changing Your Mind.* He writes, "Many of us tend to think the same thoughts, have the same feelings, and follow the same routines in our life. The rub is, this causes us to keep using the same patterns and combinations of neural circuits in our brain, and they tend to become hardwired. This is how we create habits of thinking, feeling, and doing."[25]

If you have ever tried to meditate, you might have noticed how challenging it can be to keep a still mind for longer than five seconds. As if on autopilot, our brain generates one thought after another, and unfortunately for many of us, most of those thoughts have negative connotations. For the majority of our day, we walk around having an unfavorable internal dialogue. These thoughts affect our emotions and, therefore, our moods. In turn, the way we feel can affect our body language, and we may start to slouch, put on a grim face, or cross our arms. Such behavior gives out signals to those around us that we are closed off to a connection. Through this chain of events, our thoughts can cause us to miss out on many opportunities because we are spending so much time replaying negative thought patterns in our heads. And, in most cases, we're not even aware this is happening.

As the famous motto often misattributed to Albert Einstein says, "The definition of insanity is doing the same thing over and over again and expecting different results."[26] If we keep thinking the same thoughts filled with self-criticism and judgment, isn't it absurd to expect to feel confident and happy?

---

25   Joe Dispenza, *Evolve Your Brain: The Science of Changing Your Mind* (Deerfield Beach: Health Communications, 2009).

26   "Insanity Is Doing the Same Thing Over and Over Again and Expecting Different Results," Quote Investigator, accessed February 18, 2021.

Return to Your Elevated State

Becoming conscious of negative thoughts is the first step in mind training. It's an important step because we cannot change what we are not aware of. For example, there were many moments during the process of writing this book when I became overwhelmed with negative self-talk and wanted to quit. I repeatedly questioned whether my input on these topics would be of value to anyone. I would often go online and see others talking about similar ideas I discuss in my book. Right away, my internal critic would tell me, *See? Somebody already shared everything there is to know about happiness and the process of self-discovery. Just let it go and do something else.*

This type of self-talk is common for many of us, but when we become conscious of our negative thoughts, we can start to train ourselves to disrupt them as soon as possible, making room for newer, more positive thoughts and experiences. Tony Robbins, one of the world's best transformation coaches, attributes a lot of his success to mind training. In an interview with Lewis Howes, Tony revealed that he applies what he calls the "ninety-seconds rule" throughout his day. He shared that if something upsets him, he allows himself to feel frustrated for about ninety seconds, and then he cuts it off so that a suffering state does not have a chance to consume him with negativity and snap him out of his beautiful state. He said, "If I feel the tension in me, I go, 'Okay, that's suffering. Where's it coming from?'...I noticed that the only time you have stress or suffer is when you believe a stressful thought."[27]

---

27   Tony Robbins, "7 Simple Steps to Master the Game of Money with Tony Robbins (Episode 109)," Interview by Lewis Howes, in *School of Greatness*, November 25, 2014, podcast, audio, 52:44.

Now, ninety seconds is a fantastic turnaround time to shift out of the state where something frustrates you and to move back into an elevated state where life is beautiful again. It's long enough to make the shift, but not so long that the negative emotions can affect your day. However, from my personal experience, I can attest that sometimes it takes a lot longer than ninety seconds to get back *in the zone*. It really depends on what is frustrating you and how often it arises in your life. I've realized that brushing away negative thoughts is one thing, but if they are accompanied by negative emotions it won't help to pretend that everything is okay, because those thoughts will just keep coming back. In those situations, it's important to acknowledge how you feel and, in some cases, even let those emotions take over for a little while. For example, on those days I may scream, take a nap, binge-watch Netflix shows, cry, eat pastries, or do whatever else I can do to help those emotions move through me.

Once I've let myself feel what needed to be felt, I initiate the process of returning to my elevated state. Since many things that bother us come from the mind, I find it helpful to do something that helps me take myself out of the mind and into my body. My go-to options are doing push-ups, practicing breathing exercises, dancing in a goofy way, taking a cold shower, going for a walk, shaking my body, getting a massage, singing, or even having sex.

This doesn't have to become a process that takes up your entire day. Sometimes it can take a few minutes, or sometimes a few hours. It really depends on how much is coming up on the surface for you. As long as you have a plan for how to get back to your elevated state, your negative thoughts will no longer dictate the outcome of your day. It takes willpower to remain conscious and continually disrupt the negative self-talk, but once you get a hold of it, you'll stop giving away your power to your internal critic. The negative voice may still be there, but you'll just keep doing your thing anyway. Eventually, it will get bored with you and will stop bothering you so much.

Eliminate Anything That Stands in Your Way of Becoming Your Best

When we are not busy battling our internal critic, we can redirect more energy to focus on our dreams. We can capture more opportunities because we are fully present and ready to take action without overthinking it. I'm sure most of us have come across individuals who are fully present and seem to capture everyone's attention with their radiating energy. Such people are usually very charismatic, have a confident posture, and maintain eye contact when talking to others. You actually feel they are listening to you instead of just waiting for their turn to speak. Whenever I have the pleasure of sharing the company of such people, I always feel safe and relaxed.

My mentor in public speaking, Bo Eason, is one of such people. Every time he enters a room or goes up on a stage, he takes control of the environment, and people start to feel comfortable. Bo is a master storyteller, and he helps people eliminate obstacles on their way to becoming their best and getting what they want most in life. He firmly believes that one of the key elements on the path to accomplishing our dreams is the story we tell ourselves to support that dream. In his recent book, *There's No Plan B for Your A-Game: Be the Best in the World at What You Do*, Bo shares that our goal should be to focus every day on making our story happen and eliminating anything that stands in the way. He writes, "It doesn't matter what you want to do. It only matters what story you tell yourself and then how you live out that story, every single day, until you gain mastery."[28]

When Bo was nine years old, he picked up a crayon and drew up a twenty-year plan to become the best NFL safety in the world. He was so set on accomplishing his dream that it became his proclamation. Bo probably didn't envision that forty-six years later he would be on stages worldwide, displaying this little drawing and teaching people how to master the story they tell themselves. Not only did his vision come true—he went on to play safety for the Houston Oilers, now known as the Tennessee Titans—but he also became an acclaimed playwright and actor, a best-selling author, and one of the best motivational speakers in the world.

Bo's commitment and respect for the stories that shape our lives came from his supportive parents. He grew up on a ranch and was the youngest of six kids. His dad was a real-life cowboy, and every morning he would wake his sons by whispering in their ear, "Keep moving, partner. You're the best in there, goddammit. You're the best." Bo heard that encouraging affirmation every single morning, and his dad continually repeated this declaration throughout the day too. Even though it felt uncomfortable at times, it helped Bo

---

28   Bo Eason, *There's No Plan B for Your A-Game: Be the Best in the World at What You Do* (New York: St. Martin's Press, 2019).

reinforce his story of being the best, and he kept that mindset for every pursuit he embarked on.

When I was part of Bo Eason's Warrior Mastermind group, he shared a story about how serious his mom was about his dream of becoming the best NFL safety in the world. Both he and his brother, Tony, had a dream of playing professional football, but they didn't know any pro football players and no professional athlete had ever come from their school. When they were in high school, both brothers thought they were pretty good at football, but no one else felt that way, and sadly no colleges wanted to recruit them.

One afternoon, their teammate's' parents came to their house, and someone had mentioned that the NFL was an extremely competitive sport. They went on to say it would be almost impossible to get drafted to a pro team. With all the best intentions, they had expressed that perhaps the boys should have a fallback plan, a plan B to their dreams, so that they wouldn't get their hearts broken.

Without further hesitation, Bo's mom, Mary, got up and physically escorted those guests to the front door, pushed them out onto the porch, and slammed the door behind them. His mom knew that challenges would present themselves along the way, especially while pursuing a dream of becoming an NFL player since that had a probability similar to that of getting struck by lightning. But Mary wanted her sons to remain focused on their vision, and she attempted to eliminate any distractions on their way to success. By the way, Bo's brother, Tony, was also drafted into the NFL and became a quarterback for the New England Patriots and later went on to play for the New York Jets.

There are millions of examples of kids who had supportive parents and were told that they were the best but didn't become professional athletes. Many of them didn't even make it to college athletics. Bo's story is a unique tale of various elements synchronizing to create a perfect environment for success. But he shares his story because he believes it's possible to align those elements and create the ideal setting for when an opportunity presents itself. One of those elements is creating a supportive environment. Even if your parents were not fully on board with your dreams, you can still surround yourself with friends and colleagues who believe in you and who motivate you to keep going when times get tough.

The mind is where all of the magic takes place. It's where Bo Eason crafts the story that supports his dreams and makes them a reality. It's where Tony Robbins trains himself to become conscious of his thoughts and disrupt them as soon as they take him away from his elevated state. Your mind is your home gym, and just like any training facility, it requires you to put in some effort. The first rule of your mind-training gym is to take responsibility for your inner state. Will you give away your power and allow others to determine your mood, or will you choose how you want to react in a particular situation? While it's true that we cannot always control what happens to us, we can surely train ourselves to respond in a way that supports our growth.

CHAPTER EXERCISE:
INTRODUCE SOMETHING NEW INTO YOUR DAY

Welcome to your private mind-gym! Place your journal by your side. Close your eyes and take three deep breaths. Breathe in through your nose and out through your mouth. Take a few moments to look back at the past week and think about all of the activities you conducted on autopilot. These could be things like getting dressed, brushing your teeth, working out at the gym, driving to work, or cooking breakfast. In your journal, write anything that comes to your mind.

Next, select one autopilot activity and brainstorm new elements you could introduce into your day to break up that habitual behavior. For example, you could take a new route to work, join a different workout class, or do something as simple as brushing your teeth with your non-dominant hand. For the next few weeks, I invite you to bring this new element into your day, helping you create new neural pathways in your brain.

As a second part of the exercise, make a list of your negative talk and self-criticism. What do you repeat to yourself throughout the day? Then brainstorm a more inspiring story you can introduce to replace the continuous negative self-talk, criticism, and judgment. You could say to yourself that you are lazy, incompetent, or unlucky and repeat that all day until it's ingrained in you. Or you can switch up the tune and try something different that will instill more positivity and confidence into your day. The choice is up to you.

Keep in mind that it can be quite challenging—if not impossible—to rid yourself of every negative thought, but it's much easier to replace them with uplifting ones. First, set a goal to notice when you're trapped in a loop of negative thinking. Then, interrupt those thoughts and replace them with empowering affirmations. Take the list of your negative self-talk and rewrite it with uplifting affirmations instead. Carry this piece of paper with you to refer back to these affirmations until you have them memorized.

Here's an example of the positive affirmations that have helped me along the way:

- I'm supported everywhere I go.
- I love the lessons I'm learning.
- I'm grateful for everythingI have in my life.
- I'm free to choose the best for myself.
- Life is happening *for* me, not *to* me.

CHAPTER 8:

THE SPIRITUAL PATH

"The spiritual path—is simply the journey of living our lives. Everyone is on a spiritual path; most people just don't know it."

—MARIANNE WILLIAMSON

An ancient fable tells the story of six blind men who had never seen an elephant and how they encountered one on their journey. Each man gathered around a different part of the animal and started touching it. The first man felt the tusk of the elephant and described the animal as being sharp as a spear. The second man grabbed the elephant's long trunk and described the creature as being similar to a snake. The third man touched the elephant's leg and said the animal was sturdy like a pillar or the trunk of a tree. The fourth man placed his hand on the animal's ear and said it was like some kind of a fan. The fifth man leaned against the elephant's side and said it was like a mighty wall. Finally, the sixth man pulled on the elephant's tail and said the creature reminded him of a rope.[29]

When they heard each other describe the elephant in entirely different ways, the men started arguing and yelling at one another. Each of them was certain about their own experience and held it as the absolute truth. None of the blind men were aware that they were all correct and had each experienced different aspects of the same creature. Yet they were set on proving to one another what each of them thought was valid. They clung to their version of reality, even though it was limited by their own experience and lack of perception.

This story makes an excellent point about the uniqueness of a person's experience and how real it is for each individual. Many people have a limited perception of the big picture, just a glance, yet they are so sure about their experience that they will stand behind it and even force it upon other people. I see the spiritual path as the elephant from this fable—something we can each approach from many directions and have a different encounter than someone else may have. We are all connected to one essence, one great experience.

This experience is your journey of self-discovery, the journey of getting to know your true essence and discovering what's underneath the surface. The deeper you go, the more you'll realize there is something divine within you. You just have to peel the onion to get closer to your core and closer to experiencing the miracle of life. The spiritual path is not

---

29   John Godfrey Saxe and Paul Galdone, *The Blind Men and the Elephant* (New York: McGraw-Hill, 1963).

about meditating in a perfect lotus position, reading mantras, or doing sun salutations at dawn. You don't have to live at a Hindu monastery or attend plant medicine ceremonies in Peru.

Some people walk this path by being good parents and doing their best for their kids. Others walk the path through their work, whether it's repairing cars, cooking food, or providing excellent customer service at a bank. What truly matters is how you show up to do what you do. Every moment is a new opportunity to choose. One of my teachers said the world is full of many colors, and as artists, we get to choose which colors we want to paint with. You can paint your life canvas with dark and muted colors, and you can also pick up some bright colors to liven things up.

The spiritual path is about living with intention; it's about seeking clarity about who you are and what your inner truth is. It entails being true to yourself, standing by what you believe in, and choosing that path every single day despite the obstacles you may encounter along the way. This path invites you to connect with the divine guidance. Allow it to lead you on your life's journey, even if it doesn't always make sense. Especially when it doesn't make sense.

Steve Jobs, chief executive officer and cofounder of Apple and Pixar, said in his 2005 Stanford commencement speech that we can't connect the dots looking forward; we can only connect them looking backward. He said, "You have to trust the dots will somehow connect in your future. You have to trust in something—your gut, destiny, life, karma, whatever—because believing that the dots will connect down the road will give you the confidence to follow your heart even when it leads you off the well-worn path, and that will make all of the difference."[30]

To experience that level of trust, you need to have faith and surrender to divine guidance. Such a form of surrender could actually take you out of your comfort zone, but it will guide you to where you really need to be. You may have to sacrifice your own desires for the greater good. There is an old parable about a man who was so upset about the conflict, hunger, and suffering on the planet that he raised his arms to the sky and yelled to God, "Look at this mess. Look at all this pain and suffering. Oh, God! *Why don't you do something?*" To which God responded that He did; He had sent him.

Let Your Emotions Flow Through You

On your path to discovering who you are, it's essential to let go of everything you are not. When I sat down to interview my meditation teacher, Scott Schwenk, he shared that our inability to properly process our emotions can prevent us from experiencing our true nature. "When it comes to processing emotions, we need to give ourselves a lot more compassion and feel what we're feeling without adding to it. Suppressed anger can convert into a lot of pain in the lower back or cause liver issues. According to Chinese medicine, sadness, if not processed properly, can really wreak havoc on the colon and lungs," Scott said.

---

30 Steve Jobs, "'You've Got To Find What You Love,' Jobs Says," (address presented on June 12, 2005 at the Stanford University Commencement, Stanford, CT).

Scott shared that the first step to processing emotions is to slow yourself down through conscious breath. If your mind is spinning and you feel anxiety arising in your body, it can become challenging to see things as they are. Once you slow your mind and take the story out of why you think you may be angry, sad, or afraid, you can see that it's nothing more than energy that has gotten stuck and needs to keep flowing through you. Scott emphasized that we have the right to feel whatever arises. He said that emotions don't turn us into good or bad people; rather, we are defined by how we handle those emotions.

"There's nothing bad about anger. It's a motivating force that can be used well. But when I start to project anger at somebody, that's when I start creating karma I don't want. I'm setting energy into motion. I'm putting causes and conditions for more unpleasantness into motion as I direct anger at another person or blame them for my fear or sadness. It's going to come back again and again. That's why the Buddhists talk about the wheel of suffering; the wheel of birth and death that keeps turning. The whole idea is to recognize that, see the causes, and get off the wheel," Scott shared.

In his book, *A New Earth: Awakening to Your Life's Purpose*, Eckhart Tolle, a *New York Times* best-selling spiritual author, shared an observation he had about the way animals deal with emotions. One day, he was sitting by a pond and watched two ducks get into a fight. It was a very brief dispute, after which both of them went separate ways. As they floated off, they flapped their wings to shake off the excess energy that had built up during the fight, and then they carried on in their peaceful existence. Eckhart Tolle used this example to illustrate that if the duck had a human mind, he would have created an entire story around this dispute. He would have thought that the other duck didn't respect his private space and would have come up with a plan for retaliation.

"And in this way, the duck's mind spins its tale, still thinking and talking about it, days, months, or even years later. He may never see his adversary again, but that doesn't matter. The single incident has left its impression and now has a life of its own deep within the duck's mind. As far as his body is concerned, the fight is still continuing, and the energy his body generates in response to the imaginary fight is emotion, which in turn generates more thinking," said Tolle.[31]

This is how a vicious circle of negative thinking begins. Emotions feed the story, and in return, the story fuels more emotions. Unless the duck figures out a way to take himself out of the story and realize that the fight is over, his mind will create more emotional turmoil that will disrupt his inner peace.

Stop Comparing and Judging

Indulging in behaviors like comparing, judging, and complaining prevents many people from experiencing their true selves and creates obstacles on their path. I've filled my life with a lot of suffering due to continual comparisons. Comparing has been an enormous source of negative thinking that has prevented me from respecting, appreciating, and ultimately loving myself. I would constantly compare how

---

31 Eckhart Tolle, *A New Earth: Awakening to Your Life's Purpose* (London: Penguin Books, 2018).

I did things in the past to how I was doing them in that moment. Of course, comparing can serve as a motivating function and point you in a direction where there is room for improvement. However, that works if it is performed in moderation, as a practice to utilize as a compass for checking in rather than allowing it to become a form of self-abuse.

Comparison can manifest in various ways. Some people can be overconfident and think they are better than everyone else. In contrast, others can experience the opposite effect and believe that everybody else is better off than they are. In either case, you're not fully yourself, and that can drain your energy. When you compare your self-image against other people's images, it loses its authenticity, especially in this time of glamorous displays on social media. Comparing yourself to a fabricated snapshot of somebody's life is always a dead end.

When your mind is continually evaluating your experience and putting labels on it, it is difficult to enjoy the experience for what it is. The judgment of the moment takes the magic out of it. Your attempt to label an experience as "good" or "bad" prevents you from being in the present moment and enjoying life as it is. Indian philosopher Jiddu Krishnamurti once said, "The ability to observe without evaluating is the highest form of intelligence." His work focused on understanding the nature of the mind, and he continually stressed the need for a revolution in every person's psyche.

Krishnamurti encouraged people to free themselves from constantly evaluating an experience and creating labels for it. "Do you know that even when you look at a tree and say, 'That is an oak tree,' or 'That is a banyan tree,' the naming of the tree, which is botanical knowledge, has so conditioned your mind that the word comes between you and actually seeing the tree? To come in contact with the tree, you have to put your hand on it, and the word will not help you to touch it," said Krishnamurti.[32] Liberating yourself from judging the experience can be a massive step toward experiencing more inner peace and connecting with your true essence.

The spiritual path is your life's journey. It may look very different for each person, but it leads to the same destination for each of us. We are all walking this path. The difference is that some people are unaware they are on the path while others walk it consciously. When we are unconscious on our path, we grow competitive and, as a result, become closed off from the world around us. We get distracted by our overthinking minds and the negative stories they so often create about everything that's happening around us. These stories cultivate disturbing emotions, which in return may cause unpleasant bodily sensations. When we are unconsciously living our lives, we focus on solving external problems instead of looking inward and prioritizing our inner peace.

A vital part of consciously walking this path consists of continually seeking a state of inner peace. In that state, there is no stress. There's nothing you need to prove and nothing you need to resolve—there's just pure existence. When we finally stop being in conflict with ourselves and the world around us, we can connect to our true essence.

---

32   Jiddu Krishnamurti, *Freedom from the Known* (London: Ebury Digital, 2010).

CHAPTER EXERCISE:
COMING BACK TO YOUR TRUE ESSENCE

A technique that has been helping me lately to come back to a more conscious path is practicing not identifying with the mind. It works great when you find yourself stressed out and events seem to get out of your control. It only takes a few minutes, but it can really help you regain your inner peace.

Find a comfortable position to sit or lay down and take a few deep breaths followed by a few moments of silence. Let each breath take you deeper into your inner space. Start to observe your thoughts and highlight the one that bothers you the most— a thought or an idea that carries the most charge for you at the moment. Continue to breathe calmly and say to yourself, *"I have thoughts, but I am not these thoughts."* Repeat this phrase several times. With each exhale, release the pressure and irritation caused by the thought. With each inhale, invite more relaxation and ease into your inner space.

Next, shift your attention to the chest area and start to observe the emotions that arise in you at this moment. Continue to breathe naturally and choose the emotion that causes the most uneasiness in you. Observe this feeling and say to yourself, *"I have emotions, but I am not these emotions."* Repeat this a few times until you start to feel even more relaxed.

Finally, shift your awareness to the abdomen area and observe your sensations there. Do you feel any tension or discomfort? Place your attention on your belly and begin to breathe. Let your belly rise with each inhale and descend with each exhale. Select the sensation that is the most intense at the moment and say to yourself, *"I have sensations, but I am not these sensations."* Repeat this phrase a few more times while continuing to let go of the unpleasant sensation as you exhale.

This exercise helps you experience yourself as the space that contains thoughts, emotions, and sensations. You are this formless space that is unimaginably larger than whatever it holds inside. Practice expanding this awareness as often as possible, and you will become more conscious on your path.

CHAPTER 9:

REMEMBER TO HAVE FUN

———

"We are game-playing, fun-having creatures,
we are the otters of the universe."

—RICHARD BACH

When I was nine years old, almost out of the blue, my dad said, "Son, you're going to be a tennis player." At the time, I had no idea what tennis was, but I didn't have any other plan, so I went along with his agenda. My dad was thrilled to be involved in this new project of crafting me into a professional tennis player. As time went on, I started dedicating more and more time to tennis. I had a rigorous coach, and his intentions were quite serious too.

Eventually, tennis took over schoolwork on my priority list, and I started spending a lot more time on the tennis court than in a classroom. I had an early morning practice before school, and right after my afternoon classes, my dad would pick me up and drive me to another tennis practice. Meanwhile, all of my buddies were hanging out and playing games at the park.

As tennis started to invade every aspect of my life, I began dreading going to practice. I wanted to hang out with my friends and have fun with other kids instead of spending four hours every day on the tennis court, hitting tennis balls and getting yelled at by my coach. Quite early in life, I was taught that I would need to make sacrifices if I wanted to make something of myself, so I accepted the loss of fun with my friends as one of such sacrifices.

I ended up playing tennis for the next twelve years. There were many ups and downs on this journey, and tennis played a huge role in where I am today, but I never got over the fact that it wasn't fun for me. When I finally gathered enough courage to quit, I still had no clue what I wanted to do in life, but I was certain that I didn't want to be a tennis player anymore.

When I walked away from tennis, I believed that success required sacrifices and that life was not about having fun. I continued to carry this limiting belief into my college years and later into my professional life. I had determined that fun was a distraction and that I should focus on becoming successful instead. Even when I did something fun, I couldn't fully enjoy it because I felt that I didn't deserve it. I carried my self-punishment whip with me everywhere I went.

I'd find myself watching the most beautiful sunset while sipping a glass of wine, but deep inside I felt like a lazy bum because I thought I should be doing something productive instead. Even during the most epic road trips, I managed to find time for negative self-talk to remind myself that I was still very far from reaching my professional goals and that I should feel guilty for enjoying myself. So, even though I was doing fun things, I wasn't experiencing much joy.

The way I see it, fun is incomplete without joy. It's possible to experience a state of joy without engaging in any activity, but it's quite challenging to have fun without joy. Fun involves action; it's an exciting activity that we choose to engage in. Most often, joy is a primary state or a feeling that we experience during that activity. My issue was that I did lots of exciting things, but I wasn't able to experience joy because I was so attached to the limiting belief that I didn't deserve to have fun until I became successful. It's like eating your favorite dessert but focusing on the calories you're consuming rather than fully enjoying the flavors.

Instead of having fun, I was obsessed with discipline. I developed various rituals throughout my day that were supposed to help me stay focused on achieving my goals. I took cold showers, exercised, meditated, repeated positive affirmations, and listened to audiobooks. I participated in various thirty-day challenges where I eliminated alcohol, sugar, and carbs. After I finished one challenge, I would move on to another one. My intentions were good; I wanted to be more productive and eliminate distractions on my way to success. I was continually working on my discipline and keeping myself in shape. But somehow, in this process, I had failed to notice that I was not having much fun and I was actually quite unhappy. Looking back at that experience, I realized it turned out to be self-abuse rather than something good for my personal growth and expansion.

You Don't Need a Reason to "Deserve" Fun

I experienced an "aha" moment when I got a glimpse of what fun and joy look like together. It happened during my first solo trip to Bali, Indonesia. It was my first week there, and I was still unfamiliar with the culture. My previous experiences in developing countries had taught me to stay alert, look out for pickpockets, and decline offers that sound too good to be true. On my way to the hotel, I walked by many motorbike taxi drivers who offered to give me a ride. They were lined up one after another along the road, and I kept going past them, avoiding eye contact and declining their offers. The sun was going down, I was still jet-lagged, and I did not want to engage with anyone.

Suddenly, I heard another offer for a bike taxi, and for some reason, I stopped. I wasn't sure what had changed in that moment, but I just stopped and said hello to the taxi driver in front of me. He was an older man, probably half my size, but his eyes radiated with energy. I told him that I didn't need a ride back to the hotel, but I was open to exploring new places the following day. My own answer stunned me. *I just agreed to ride on a motorbike with someone I met just a few seconds ago!*

When I told the man that I wanted to explore, his face lit up with the biggest smile I've ever seen. In his broken English, he expressed how glad he was that I had stopped to talk to him and how much this job meant for him. I didn't know what to make of it all at the time. I was still quite surprised by my reaction, but I wanted to see new sites and felt like helping this guy out. We agreed that he'd take me to a few nearby beaches the following day, and I went back to my hotel. The rest of the way, I walked with a completely different attitude and energy. I smiled at the people who kept offering bike rides. I was happy that I had listened to my intuition and did something I normally wouldn't do. I was thrilled about this new adventure.

The following morning, I finished breakfast and walked out of the hotel to find my new friend waiting on his bike with two helmets for us. When he saw me, he was happy I had shown up. He thanked me again for giving him a job and shared that when I had met him the night before, he was sad because he couldn't afford to buy offerings for the upcoming Hindu holiday. He teared up and told me that he was so happy he had found a job for the day and that he and his family could properly celebrate their holiday.

That entire day, I felt so much joy in riding with this happy old man and exploring the most beautiful beaches I'd ever seen. I took a selfie of us cruising on his bike, and I later noticed I had the biggest smile on my face. It definitely wasn't because I had finally attained success and felt like I now deserved to have fun. Quite the opposite, actually. I had come to Bali right after I shut down the swimsuit company I'd been working on for a few years. I was embarrassed, disappointed in myself, and felt like a total failure. Yet there I was, experiencing joy and having fun on the back of that motorbike.

Recently, I revisited that photo and noticed that the T-shirt I wore that day had Andrew Murphy's quote, "You are confined only by the walls you build yourself."

I still don't have a logical explanation for why this happened that way. Based on my internal algorithm, I was supposed to deserve to have fun and be joyous only when I had attained success. Yet there I was, a total failure but happy. It's as if I had finally given in and stopped trying to prove wrong to my "internal abuser"" who was constantly beating myself up, and I had said, *Yes, I'm a failure. I don't deserve it, but I'll do it anyway. I will have fun and experience joy. I will eat the cake and taste its sweetness without worrying about the calories.* I had finally allowed myself to have fun, and joy had joined the party.

On our way back to the hotel, my new friend said he wanted to stop by his home and introduce me to his family. I was a little hesitant but accepted his invitation. His family lived in a small house, which he had probably built himself. When we pulled up, his wife came out with their kids to greet us, and she expressed her gratitude for giving her husband a job that day. As we prepared to head back, the man's wife gave me a few pieces of fruit she had prepared as part of their offering for the upcoming holiday. Now it was my turn to tear up.

As I sat on the back of the bike, I contemplated how much had happened because something inside me told me to stop and talk to that man. That encounter helped me rewire and view fun not as a distraction, but as a vital component to experiencing life more fully. My battle with limiting beliefs still continues, and once in a while I still struggle with allowing myself to have fun, but I am a lot more aware of it now.

Fun Is a Gateway to Creativity

Albert Einstein once said that creativity is intelligence having fun.[33] Fun involves play, and play requires spontaneity. So how can we be more spontaneous in our day-to-day tasks? We all have different ways of managing our lives. There is time for nurturing rituals and discipline, and also time for spontaneity and play. Many of us live in fast-paced environments, and we don't have lots of free time to explore the world and look for adventures to strengthen our relationship with fun. We have to be considerate of our responsibilities while allowing some room for fun between our strict schedules and deadlines.

We can plan fun ahead of time, and spontaneity will come into play during the activity. For example, one of my friends likes to go rock climbing, but he has a busy work schedule. So, he plans his fun ahead of time, and when he gets on the mountain, he unleashes his inner child and becomes spontaneous and playful.

There's a reason why so many successful start-up offices look like theme parks these days. You can find skate parks, basketball courts, rock walls, Olympic-size pools, sleep pods, gourmet chefs, anything that can keep employees happy and boost their engagement at work. For instance, Dropbox,

---

33   "Creativity is intelligence having fun," A Quote by Albert Einstein. Goodreads, accessed April 29, 2021.

a file-hosting service platform, built a jam room for their employees—a music room equipped with keyboards, guitars, drums, and various other instruments to uplift the mood and boost the creativity of their workforce. Similarly, offices at GoDaddy, the domain registrar and web-hosting company, have an indoor racetrack for pedal go-karts so their employees can have fun with each other and engage in play throughout the day. Plenty of research has shown that people who are more active are overall happier and much more engaged at work.

One of my mentors said that we gain access to great ideas when we are having fun. We can tap into our creative juices when we lose track of time while engaging in an activity we are passionate about. That could be singing, dancing, working on your car, teaching on stage, jumping out of an airplane, playing sports, and so many other activities that help you stay in the present moment and keep you in your body and out of your head.

Many artists, entrepreneurs, and innovators credit their work with an intervention of a higher force or, as some of them call it, their muse. Ideas come to them while they're playing sports, walking in nature, playing with their kids, or even while taking a shower. They feel inspired when they are fully engaged in an activity and are able to put their analytical minds aside to let something greater than themselves take over. Is it God, the Universe, or Spirit? This is open to individual interpretation. What's important is that they trust and surrender with humility, and they allow themselves to become vessels to manifest beautiful creations in the physical world.

CHAPTER EXERCISE:
LET'S HAVE FUN

An exercise that has helped me bring more fun into my life is to take a complete inventory of everything that makes me feel joyful and excited. When I first entered all of this in my journal, two things happened. First, I noticed that my list was surprisingly short. Second, I saw that the items on my list appeared on my schedule only once in a while. Right away, I knew what I needed to do to include more fun into my life, and I invite you to do this exercise as well.

In your journal, list any activities you feel excited about such as hiking, dancing, clearing out your garage, painting, or working out. If it is challenging to think of things that currently excite you, consider what activities you were excited about as a child. Now look at your list and circle the top five that you feel could be the most fun for you right now. Experiment by engaging in these activities more often for the next few weeks and note in your journal any changes in your overall mood.

Remember, you don't have to shoot straight for the stars by trying to find something that will take your breath away. It's important to train your *joy muscle,* and a great start is to learn how to observe your body and notice during which activities you start losing track of time. I'm not talking about an hour slipping by while you watch YouTube videos of funny cats (guilty as charged). I'm referring to getting lost in drawing, dancing, or building sandcastles, something you would do often even if you already had all of the money you needed to live a care-free life.

CHAPTER 10:

ACCEPT YOUR UNIQUENESS

—

"Our job in this lifetime is not to shape ourselves into some ideal we imagine we ought to be, but to find out who we already are and become it."

—STEVEN PRESSFIELD

When I was seven, I used to tie a rope around a broom and pretend it was my guitar. My grandma gathered her friends, and as part of our evening entertainment, I sang and danced for everyone. I enjoyed entertaining, and they seemed to enjoy it as well because it was a weekly gig I had for the entire duration of my summer in the countryside. I never moved on to playing real instruments or finding out whether I had any musical talent. The following year, my dad signed me up to play tennis, and the next twelve years of my life I spent hitting tennis balls for hours a day.

I've heard so many stories from different people about their childhood dreams and how they wanted to become musicians, dancers, designers, athletes, or entrepreneurs. But as time went on, their dreams got mixed up with the suggestions from their parents, teachers, and friends, and they never followed through with their initial intentions. Unfortunately, as we get older, many people stop listening to their inner voices and instead start shaping their decisions based on other people's opinions and their environment.

The Art of Being Yourself

Caroline McHugh, the founder and CEO of IDOLOGY, has dedicated the past two decades of her life to helping individuals worldwide uncover the original versions of themselves. She encourages people to let go of their approval addiction and a constant need to be recognized by other people. "Living somebody else's opinion and mistaking it for your own is one of the most debilitating things you'll do on the road to being yourself. You will never ever be perception-less, but it's important to be perception-free," said Caroline.[34] In her famous TEDx Talk, "The Art of Being Yourself," Caroline shared two stages in life when we are the most connected to our uniqueness—when we are young and when we are old. "It's kind of like an hourglass effect—when you're young, you're great at being yourself; when you're old, you're great at being yourself. But the bit in the middle is sometimes the most problematic. That's about where you have to socialize,

---

34   Caroline McHugh, "The Art of Being Yourself," Filmed February 2013 at TEDxMiltonKeynesWomen, Milton Keynes, UK, video, 26:23.

you have to accommodate, you have to adapt," shared Caroline.

She inspires people to become adventurous and explore their uniqueness without worrying about what others around them may think. Caroline's observations led her to believe that people who embraced themselves stand out in the crowd, and in many instances, the ones who are afraid to be themselves end up working for the ones who are not.

In her talk, she shared a story about an important lesson she learned about humility when she was still a little girl. Caroline said that humility was not thinking less of yourself; rather, it was thinking about yourself less. She grew up in Glasgow, Scotland, in a working-class family. Nobody had any money at that time, and they couldn't afford to go out and get entertained, so instead, they gathered at each other's homes, drank, and sang songs.

Caroline shared that even though most of these folks were welders and carpenters by day, they turned into Frank Sinatra, Dean Martin, and Sarah Vaughn at night. All the kids were taught to perform as well. Caroline and her sisters frequently brought their guitar downstairs and sang for the guests. She said that they were not any good at all, but that didn't matter to anyone.

One evening, it was time to sing again, but Caroline was dreading the event. When her mom came up to her room, she told her that she was shy, that everybody looked at her and she didn't want to sing anymore. Her mom smiled and said, "Caroline, don't flatter yourself, darling. Do you think anybody downstairs is interested in you? They're not. Your job is to go downstairs and make them happy, so go and sing." With a sense of relief, Caroline picked up her sisters and her guitar and went downstairs to sing for the guests.

That experience helped Caroline achieve a spectacular disregard for being the center of attention. She realized that it wasn't about her; it was about the guests in their living room. From that day on, she made her audience the center of her attention. While the core of Caroline's work is helping people discover their uniqueness, she emphasizes that it's not always about them but their role in a much larger design.

Your Self-Expression Is the Greatest Gift to the World

"Just be yourself!" is the most frustrating advice I've ever gotten. Every time I heard it, I was filled with despair because I had no clue who I was. I always envied people who, from a very young age, knew what they wanted to do in life. While traveling in Nepal, I met a guy who told me that he used to build little toy airplanes from as early as he could remember. As he got older, his dad brought him more complex airplane models to put together. Finally, when it was time to go to college, he studied to become an aeronautical engineer, and then Boeing Company recruited him to build airplanes for them.

When he told me this story, I became quite upset. I was thirty years old at that time, with a few unsuccessful attempts at finding my calling in life. I went all the way to Nepal to "find myself," and here was this guy telling me that he knew what he was meant to do from the time he was three years old.

Ethan Hawke, an American actor, writer, and director, talked about the importance of self-discovery and expressing your uniqueness to the world. "If you want to help your community, if you want to help your family, if you want to help your friends, you have to express yourself. And to express yourself, you have to know yourself. It's actually super easy. You just have to follow your love. There is no path. There's no path until you walk it. And you have to be willing to play the fool," said Ethan.[35] He emphasized that once you get close to what you love, who you are is revealed to you, and it starts to expand.

Of course, we may experience resistance and fear when we move closer to something important to us—an experience that can help us evolve and become the greatest value to the world. Fear of our own success can even push us away from our true calling in life and drive us to sabotage our efforts. But we can also transform this dreadful feeling into our ally and use it to point us in the right direction.

Ethan sees our individuality as a vital component of humanity and a powerful tool for healing each other. He encourages us to learn to be free, like kids, and embark on various callings without thinking about whether it's good or bad for us. "That's what makes kids so beautifully creative—is

---

35   Ethan Hawke, "Give Yourself Permission to Be Creative," Filmed June 2020, TED video, 9:08.

that they don't have any habits, and they don't care if they're any good or not. They're not building a sandcastle going, 'I think I'm going to be a really good sandcastle builder.' They just throw themselves at whatever project you put in front of them," shared Ethan.

When I think about the story of my guitar concerts for my grandma and her friends, I realize that I used to be that kid in Ethan's example who didn't care whether he was any good. After all, my broom didn't even make any sounds, so who's to judge? I didn't think about my outfit or how I moved around my imaginary stage. All I cared about was my audience and making sure they were having a great time. Over the years, I have lost the ability to have such careless fun without worrying about the opinion of people around me. Somewhere along my journey, I stopped accepting who I was and became obsessed with fixing myself.

I was determined to rid myself of all of my insecurities and acquire new skills that would make me a stronger individual—a version of me I could finally respect and be proud of. Such a selective process of accepting some parts of myself while rejecting others created lots of conflict and resistance within me. I failed to understand that all of these aspects of me that I labeled as weak or as strong were still an integral part of who I was.

Accept and Forgive

You may have noticed that some people radiate energy and confidence while others dim their lights and hide. Why is that so? Could it be that some people have accepted themselves entirely while others are still trying to fix themselves? Being yourself is a real art. It's a journey of a lifetime that involves a meticulous process of self-discovery and self-mastery. On this journey, we seek to explore our uniqueness and learn to trust ourselves. We learn to accept our imperfections because they are an integral part of our identities. We work toward forgiving ourselves for unmet expectations and releasing any grudges we may hold against ourselves. The art of being ourselves requires falling in love with all the things, good and bad, that make us who we are.

I've been on a journey of self-discovery for a long time. I've dedicated time to peeling the onion layers to understand who I am not so I could finally get closer to the core of who I am. My path to self-acceptance started by forgiving myself. I realized that I held on to so many grudges against myself. I had many expectations about who I wanted to become and where I wanted to be in life. Every time I missed the mark, I got angry with myself and stuffed it deep inside.

Regrets and disappointments became excess baggage that got heavier and heavier. Quite often I rejected love from people around me because I couldn't fully accept and love myself. If we don't love ourselves in the first place, how can we accept love from others? We'll find ways to reject them and prove that we are not worthy of them. It's the most prominent form of self-sabotage. I refused to accept my failures and lived in a fantasy bubble until I finally did a reality check and witnessed things for what they really were. I admitted to myself that everything was not as picture-perfect as I imagined it to be and that I was okay with that.

One of my teachers once asked me, "What are you willing to let go of for the sake of your inner peace?" Letting go of what I wanted to become but didn't returned me to my inner peace and allowed me to start fresh. There is no other possible past, but there is every possible future. Every moment is a new moment where we can make a new choice. It's never too late to start again. Acknowledging where we stand and seeing our next step is all that's needed. The desire for self-improvement may never cease. We are all students of life, and it's essential to learn from a place of abundance where we are already whole and we have enough. It is a place where we are learning because we are curious, not because we are attempting to fix something within ourselves.

Exercising compassion toward ourselves and becoming more accepting is the key to living a life of happiness and fulfillment. When I finally befriended who I already was, I saw that my life thus far had not been a disappointment whatsoever. It's what made me interesting and allowed me to write this book. My unique experiences, both my failures and successes, had brought me to this point in my life, where I got to face myself and finally see things clearly.

CHAPTER EXERCISE:
HO'OPONOPONO

Ho'oponopono is a Hawaiian prayer for forgiveness that can help us let go of the grudges and blame we hold against ourselves as well as other people. The name of this practice roughly translates to "make things right" or "put things back into balance." Forgiving ourselves is an essential step in the process of accepting ourselves. Those parts of us that are still limited by destructive beliefs need to be recognized, accepted, and, in some cases, released.

Ho'oponopono consists of four simple phrases that are rooted in repentance, forgiveness, gratitude, and love. To gain the most from this practice, try to feel deep contact with your body when you repeat the four phrases listed below. This state of relaxation, trust, and vulnerability will help you release the tension associated with any misunderstandings, resentments, guilt, shame, and any other unpleasant feelings.

You can either find a guided Ho'oponopono meditation online and play it in the background or you can just comfortably sit and repeat the phrases to yourself. Try different options and see which one works best for you. I recommend starting this exercise with yourself and then moving on to healing your relationships with other people.

First phrase: *I'm Sorry*
The first step requires you to acknowledge that a wrong has occurred. Remember a situation when you failed to uphold your boundaries or compromised your principles, for which you later felt shame and criticized yourself. Or perhaps there are bad habits or addictions you continually beat yourself up for yet continue to indulge in them. Visualize an image of yourself or a younger version of you, give yourself a long hug, and say from the bottom of your heart, "I'm sorry."

Second phrase: *Please Forgive me*
Free yourself from the burden of guilt, shame, and regret by asking yourself for forgiveness. True forgiveness is not about forgetting the wrongdoing but acknowledging it first

and making a conscious choice to stop investing your energy there and finally moving on.

Third phrase: *Thank you*
Amid a frustrating moment when you're angry with yourself or upset at someone else, it could be challenging to remember to feel thankful. However, do you remember how many times what you thought was the worst thing that could have happened to you turned out to be the most valuable lesson in your life? Now is an excellent opportunity to remember some of those moments and connect with the healing energy of gratitude.

Fourth phrase: *I love you*
Go back to the time when you felt the most loved; when there was no judgment or disapproval—just unconditional love. Connect to this feeling with your entire body and bring it to a situation for which you feel guilty and blame yourself. Place your hands on your heart, and despite having done something you're not proud of, say, "I love you."

CHAPTER 11:

WHAT'S NEXT?

———

When I stepped on the path to self-discovery, I didn't have a clear idea of where I was headed. All I knew was that something was missing in my life. Limited thinking obstructed my perception, and instead of moving with intention, I just followed where the wind blew. Most of my decisions were shaped by the conditioning formed at a very young age.

As I thoroughly examined and contemplated many themes discussed in this book, I started to get a better picture of where I wanted to be. Interacting with many inspiring people in the field of personal development helped me better understand this journey of self-mastery.

At the beginning of this book, I mentioned that the wisest people on the planet point within as the way to true happiness, but how do we access it? How do we clear the obstacles that stand in our way of experiencing more happiness?

The path of self-discovery is filled with duality and seeming paradoxes. From one angle, there is nowhere we need to get to, nothing we need to accomplish. Happiness is already available to us at this very instant. From another angle, there are actions we can take to clear the obstacles and create more harmony within our lives so we can experience happiness. It's not the same as attaching conditions to your happiness, like *I'll be happy when I get promoted to my next role,* or *I'll be happy when we move to Costa Rica.* True happiness is not attached to anything. It's not something we need to earn. It's something that arises when we release all of the conditions and clear away all of the expectations on ourselves and our lives.

There are many ways to cultivate happiness in various aspects of our lives. One of the main messages that I hoped to convey was our ability to attract more of what we focus on. The daily awareness of this alone can profoundly affect the quality of your life.

If you made it this far into the book, you've most likely made progress with freeing yourself of the limitations that no longer serve you so you can experience more happiness. I genuinely hope that the stories within this book and the exercises at the end of each chapter help you derive more satisfaction and fulfillment from every new endeavor you embark on.

Lasting change takes time and requires consistency with your practices. The results of such work will help you become more conscious of your thoughts, emotions, and actions needed to take more responsibility for your inner state. You may notice that after using the practices mentioned in this book, you will be able to interpret the events in your life in an empowering way instead of plunging into the *victim mindset.* Remember, even the smallest changes can make a huge difference.

Every day, you have a choice to make. You can get behind the steering wheel and set an intention for the day, or you can let events just unfold and react based on what has happened. The key lies in the regular application of these concepts and ideas. Make them not just ideas you contemplate once in a while but actual rules you live by.

It's comparable to the distinction between conventional healthcare and preventive medicine. In conventional medicine, we cure the disease. In preventive, we take appropriate measures to ensure that we never get sick in the first place. I'm a big proponent of the preventive approach, and I try to apply it to as many areas in my life as I can. This approach prompts us to be more aware and pay attention to the signals that our bodies and our environment send us.

When we become more conscious of what we think, what we say, and what we do, we can have better relationships with ourselves and the people around us. When we act with intention, we will not get distracted by senseless disputes and will have fewer detours off our path.

A wise person once told me that co-creation with the Universe is a 50/50 deal. We do our part, and the Universe will take care of the rest. It's an ongoing dance of acting with intention and surrendering to a higher force.

As a farewell, I would like to leave you with one last exercise to help incorporate everything that you've read in this book.

This exercise is a letter to yourself. Write it on behalf of your future self, who implemented various practices mentioned in this book. In this letter, describe how much your life has changed as a result of this experience.

Talk about your relationships with the people around you, how you express yourself, or your new diet. If you decide to take on daily gratitude practice, mention how it may have helped you experience more abundance in your life.

Once you finish the letter, fold it into an envelope and hide it somewhere safe. In a few weeks, read it out loud and try to feel everything mentioned there as if it has already happened. Revisit this letter as often as you need to remind yourself of the intentions you have created. Connect with the feelings of gratitude for this beautiful journey of self-discovery and self-mastery that you're on, and for staying at the steering wheel of your life.

ACKNOWLEDGMENTS

———

First and foremost, I would like to thank my family for supporting all of my dreams and giving me the freedom to live my life to the fullest. To my amazing parents Svetlana and Igor Arsonov—thank you for bringing me into this world with love and care. I feel so much gratitude for the support and encouragement from my amazing sister, Anastasiya, and my badass brother, Dima.

I'm honored to have had an opportunity to learn from my incredible teachers, Scott Schwenk and Kai Karrel. Thank you for inspiring me to discover the true essence of who I am.

I am eternally grateful for the opportunity to learn from Kyle Cease, Bo Eason, and Laura Pringle, who have all played a vital part in my journey of self-mastery.

Thank you to all of the phenomenal people I interviewed on the *Think Clever* podcast. This book would not have been possible if it wasn't for your inspiring stories. Special thanks to Kristin Brabant, John Pogachar, Dr. Jeremy Goldberg, Jen Jones, Al Tutson, and Conni Biesalski.

I want to thank my publisher, New Degree Press, for believing in me and providing all of the necessary resources and expertise needed to bring this book to fruition. Thank you, Eric Koester, Brian Bias, Linda Berardelli, Avery Lockland, Tiffany Bunch, Kayla LeFevre, and of course, the rockstar marketing and revisions editor—Jason Chinchen.

I have so much appreciation for the visual genius and my fellow seeker, Vanni Mongoni.

I would like to acknowledge the early readers of my manuscript and thank them for their feedback and for helping me produce the final form of this book: Dany Ceseña, Philipp Gruendler, Stuart Clark, Irina Leonova, Brenda Gazzar, Dmitry Karpenko, Andrea Valdettaro, Ralf Wagner, Dr. Karina Klimtchuk, and Jeri Bonis.

I would also like to thank my incredible author's community, who supported me all the way and without whom this book would not be published: Igor and Leigh Morosowski, Bobby Williams, Koby Poulton, Greg and Ilona Panas, Raisa and Tanya Logacheva, Jocelyne Miranda, Josie Wilder, Genady and Tatyana Makarenko, Pavlenko Maryna, Jesper and Caroline Bergkvist, Isabel Ochoa, Lysenko Olga, Ehsan Safavi, Valery Semin, Ben Roby, Anton Brandt, Amber Zinsmeister, Pedram Vahid, Marcella Sidelnik, Dmitry Pasumansky, Laney Clark, Gayaneh Davoodian, Parsa Vahid, Rodman Amiri, Felix Dey, Alex Abramian, Andrew Quinn, Emily Olsen, Tiffany Ma, Todd Hall, Lehua Kay, Natalie Gallegos, Paolina Milana, James Armstrong, Timothy Lafolette, Sue Hahm, Thomas Moorcroft, Lindsay Apatow, Sara Isakovic, Matthew Wride, Ksenia Moore, Cristina Monti, Vanessa Fry,

Craig Whitlock, Berly Rodriguez, Michael Harding, Drake Townes-Witzel, Brady Toops, Lisa Giasi, Linda Minor, Regina Morales Izurieta, Mishayla Spendlove, Sandi Salerno, Asha Fereydouni, Irene Carrillo, Alejandra Valenzuela, Shauna Zeilig, Victoria Popov, Anthony Ryan Benedicto, Kristen Svensson, Camie Chandler, Oleksandra Ushakova, Laura Vallverdu, Aurora Fritz, Lainey Depolla, Serdar Turan, Lara Mirinjian, Ben Marciano, Jaclyn Lineback, Peter Kapich, Guy Baruch, Valerieann Giovanni, Randy Del Cid, Trey Arnold, Bobby Bluford, Daniel Cooper, Mai Ton Pai, Dawn Suits, Sasha Srivastava, Linsey Desich, Eric Wittenberg, Valerie Gray, John Ma, Felice Dubois, Elena and Tatyana Mironova, Jason Chase, Maryam Garg, Daniel Fetzner, Miguel Manalo, Angela and Nancy Ceseña, Isaac Cordova, Vladimir Salnikov, Ann Nguyen, Carlo Reitano, Mariia Liubenko, Komal Shah, Monika Rakhmanberdiyeva, Dina Rezvanipour, Mindy Goldstein, Pei Chiang, Nick Klinger, Tiffany Brewster, Alba Haya, Iris Roschitz-Dey, Bozena Čulo, Gabe Bensimon, Bert Maes, Noel Busby, Chad Tew, and Randolph Zuniga.

Finally, I want to thank Xenia for being there to listen to all of my rambling and help me make sense of it. I appreciate your patience and support throughout this journey; it helped me keep going during the challenging times.

APPENDIX

Introduction:

Tseng, J. and J. Brian Poppenk. "Meta-State Transitions Demarcate Thoughts Across Task Contexts Exposing the Mental Noise of Trait Neuroticism." *Nature Communications* 11, no. 1 (July 2020): 1-12. https://doi.org/10.1038/s41467-020-17255-9.

Chapter 1:

Arsonov, Stas. "A Very Kind Place: The LOVE Billboards." Produced by Stanislav Arsonov and directed by Angela Isabel. June 27, 2019. Video: 10:07. Accessed February 22, 2021 at https://www.youtube.com/watch?v=-O6_SkYLFz4&feature=youtu.be.

Giono, Jean. *The Man Who Planted Trees*. Boston: Shambhala, 2000.

Goldberg, Jeremy. "What If Kindness Was Cool?" Filmed May, 2015 at TEDxTownsville, Townsville, Australia. video, 17:19. https://www.youtube.com/watch?v=5mklMPHGLjo.

Redfield, James. *Celestine Prophecy*. Boston: Little, Brown & Co., 1994.

Chapter 2:

Cho, H., S. Ryu, J. Noh, and J. Lee. "The Effectiveness of Daily Mindful Breathing Practices on Test Anxiety of Students." *PLoS One* 11, no. 10, e0164822 (October 20, 2016). https://doi:10.1371/journal.pone.0164822.

Chowdhury, Madhuleena Roy. "The Neuroscience of Gratitude and How It Affects Anxiety & Grief." PositivePsychology (January 9, 2020). https://positivepsychology.com/neuroscience-of-gratitude/.

Krasno, Jeff and Scott Schwenk. "Open Your Breath, Open Your Life." February, 2019. *Commune*. Podcast. MP3 audio, 29:00. https://open.spotify.com/episode/26RYXpFfu7LEo6vBFUuP5k.

Chapter 3:

Brand, Russell. "How to NOT Ruin a Relationship." September 17, 2020. Video, 9:59. https://www.youtube.com/watch?v=7N-pRB8lOGFo.

Brown, Brené. "RSA Short: Empathy." December 10, 2013. Video, 2:53. https://youtu.be/1Evwgu369Jw.

Gibran, Kahlil. *The Prophet*. New York: Alfred A. Knopf, 1923.

Ruiz, Miguel. *The Four Agreements: A Practical Guide to Personal Freedom*. San Rafael, CA: Amber-Allen Pub., 1997.

Chapter 4:

Harter, Jim. "Dismal Employee Engagement Is a Sign of Global Mismanagement." *Gallup*, 2021. https://www.gallup.com/workplace/231668/dismal-employee-engagement-sign-global-mismanagement.aspx.

Jones, Jen. "Vasstu Architecture: An Ancient Approach for Modern Times." *Jen Jones Architecture*, March 2, 2019. https://www.jenjonesarchitecture.com/blog.

Tolle, Eckhart. *Stillness Speaks*. Novato, CA: New World Library, 2003.

Chapter 5:

"Rise early. It is the early bird that catches the worm. Don't be fooled by this absurd law; I once knew a man who tried it. He got up at sunrise and a horse bit him." Mark Twain Quotations - Early Rising, Accessed April 29, 2021. http://www.twainquotes.com/Early_rising.html.

Robbins, Tony. "7 Simple Steps to Master the Game of Money with Tony Robbins (Episode 109)." Interview by Lewis Howes, *School of Greatness*, November 25, 2014. Audio, 52:44. https://lewishowes.com/podcast/tony-robbins/.

Wattles, Wallace D. *The Science of Getting Rich: How to Make Money and Get the Life You Want*. Scotts Valley: CreateSpace, 2015.

Chapter 6:

Jin, Duo-Chen et al. "Regulation of the serotonin transporter in the pathogenesis of irritable bowel syndrome." *World Journal of Gastroenterology* vol. 22,36 (2016): 8137-48. https://doi:10.3748/wjg.v22.i36.8137

Johnson, Katerina V.-A. "Gut Microbiome Composition and Diversity Are Related to Human Personality Traits." *Human Microbiome Journal* 15 (March 2020): 1-15. https://doi.org/10.1016/j.humic.2019.100069.

Kamiya, MD, Atsushi. "The Brain-Gut Connection." *Johns Hopkins Medicine: Health*, accessed February 18, 2021. https://www.hopkinsmedicine.org/health/wellness-and-prevention/the-brain-gut-connection.

Lugavere, Max. "Dementia Is Preventable through Lifestyle." Filmed November 2, 2018 in Venice Beach, CA. TEDx video, 19:37. https://www.youtube.com/watch?v=foWCb23KPEw.

Perlmutter, David, and Kristin Loberg. *Grain Brain: The Surprising Truth about Wheat, Carbs, and Sugar—Your Brain's Silent Killers.* London: Yellow Kite, 2019.

Zhang, Sheng, and De-Chang Chen. "Facing a new challenge: the adverse effects of antibiotics on gut microbiota and host immunity." *Chinese Medical Journal* 132, no. 10. (May 20, 2019): 1135-1138.

Chapter 7:

Dispenza, Joe. *Evolve Your Brain: The Science of Changing Your Mind*. Deerfield Beach: Health Communications, 2008.

Eason, Bo. *There's No Plan B for Your A-Game: Be the Best in the World at What You Do*. New York: St. Martin's Press, 2019.

"Insanity Is Doing the Same Thing Over and Over Again and Expecting Different Results." Quote Investigator, accessed February 18, 2021. https://quoteinvestigator.com/2017/03/23/same/.

Robbins, Tony. "7 Simple Steps to Master the Game of Money with Tony Robbins (Episode 109)." Interview by Lewis Howes, *School of Greatness*, November 25, 2014. Audio, 52:44. https://lewishowes.com/podcast/tony-robbins/.

Chapter 8:

Jobs, Steve. "'You've Got To Find What You Love,' Jobs Says," *Stanford | news*. Address presented on June 12, 2005 at the Stanford University Commencement, Stanford, CT, accessed February 18, 2021. https://news.stanford.edu/2005/06/14/jobs-061505/.

Krishnamurti, Jiddu. *Freedom from the Known*. London: Ebury Digital, 2010.

Saxe, John Godfrey, and Paul Galdone. *The Blind Men and the Elephant*. New York: McGraw-Hill, 1963.

Tolle, Eckhart. *A New Earth: Awakening to Your Life's Purpose*. London: Penguin Books, 2018.

Chapter 9:

"Creativity is intelligence having fun," A Quote by Albert Einstein. Goodreads, accessed April 29, 2021.

Chapter 10:

Hawke, Ethan. "Give Yourself Permission to Be Creative." Filmed June 2020, TED video, 9:08. https://www.ted.com/talks/ethan_hawke_give_yourself_permission_to_be_creative.

McHugh, Caroline. "The Art of Being Yourself." Filmed February 2013 at TEDxMiltonKeynesWomen, Milton Keynes, UK., video, 26:23. https://www.youtube.com/watch?v=veEQQ-N9xWU&feature=emb_logo.

Made in United States
Orlando, FL
17 March 2022